PAINTING A

LOWRY

Coming from the Mill

A RECONSTRUCTION BY EDWIN BOWES

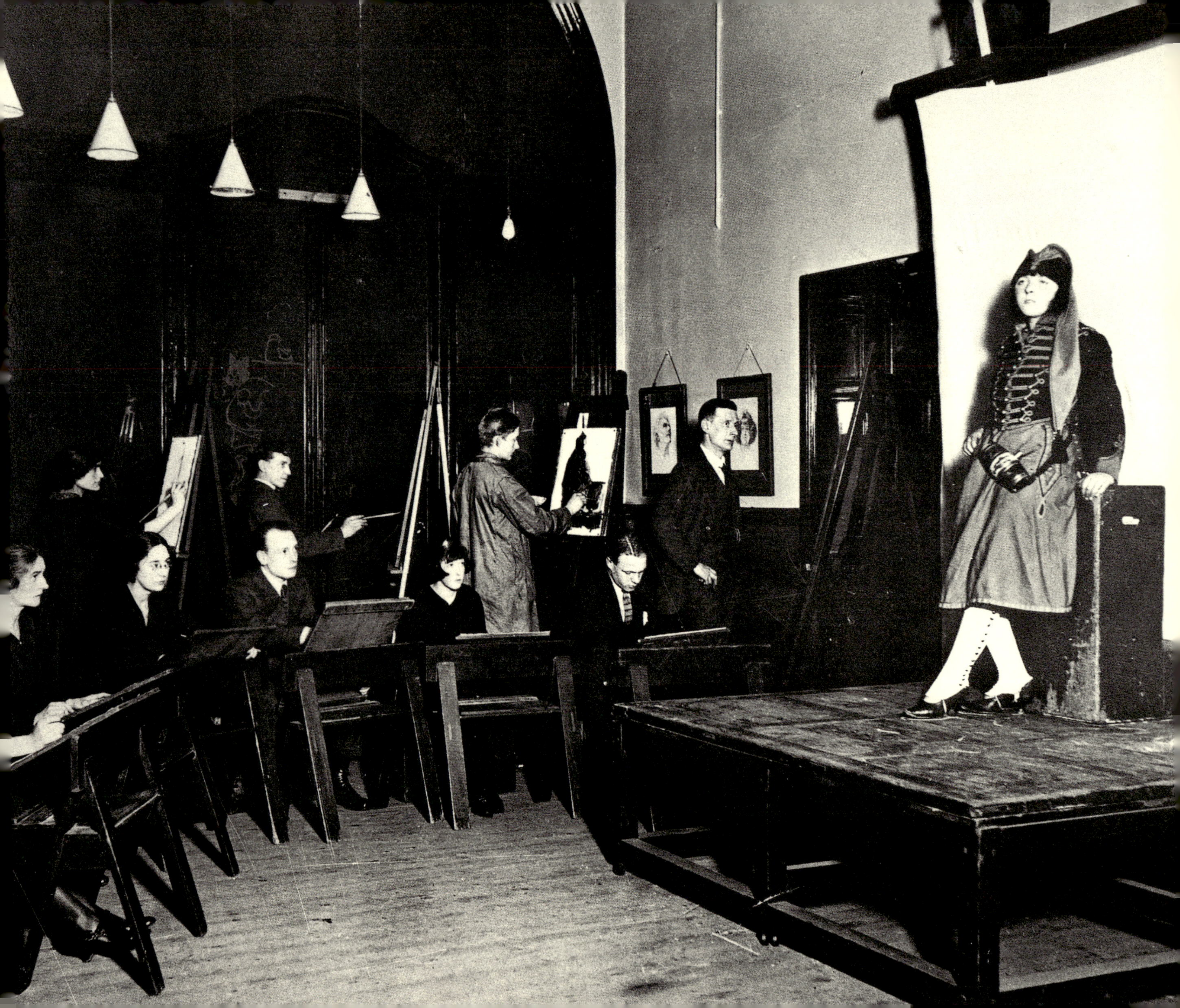

CONTENTS

Left *Lowry in the costume class at Salford School of Art around 1919. On the right of the group, he stands back from an easel implying that he may have been at work on an oil painting like the male student behind him. The students seated in the foreground may be sketching in pencil or working in watercolour.*

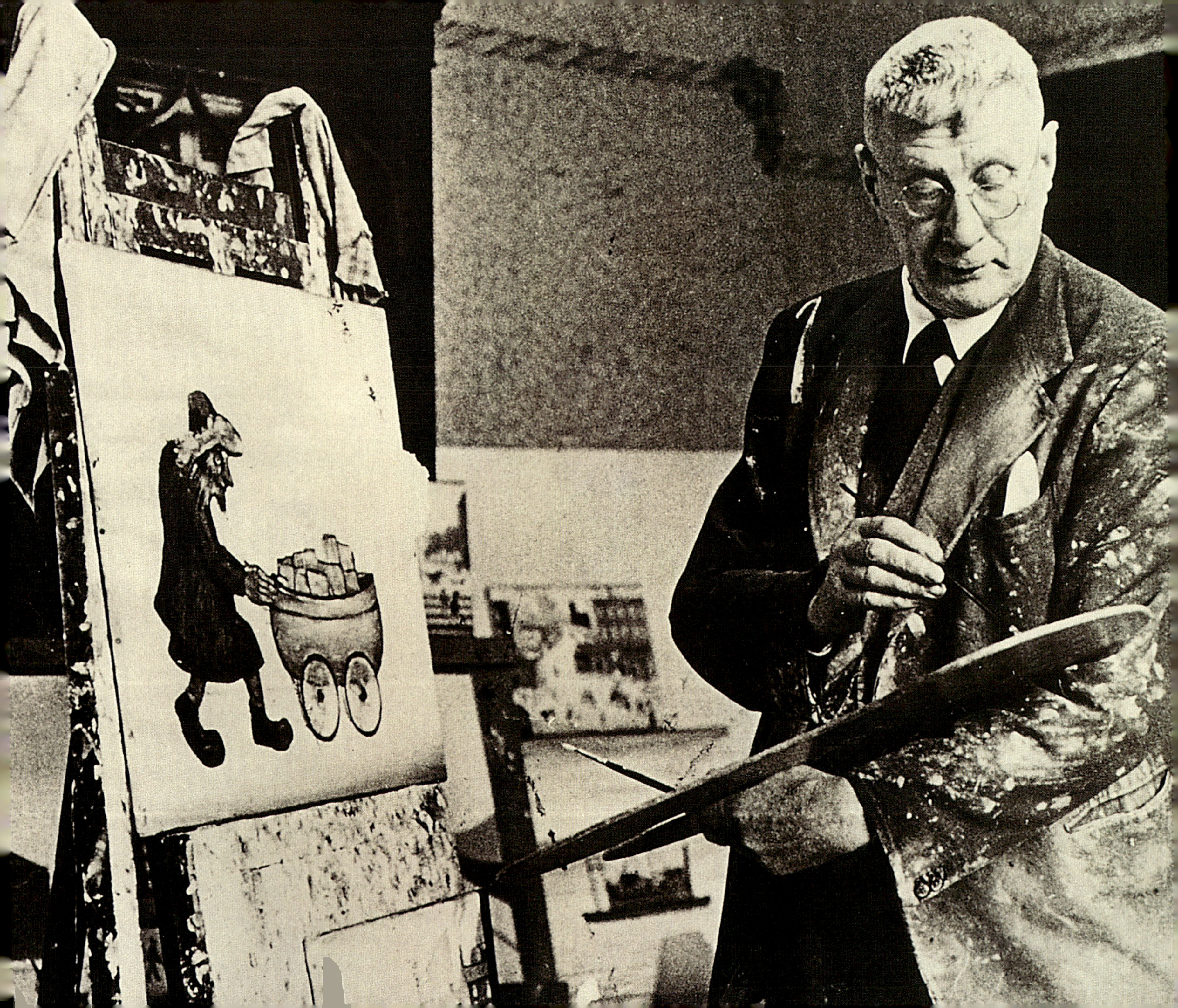

Few twentieth century British artists have been filmed at work in the studio more often than L. S. Lowry. Photographers were permitted to look over his shoulder as he painted and friends quizzed him at length about his working practices. But this wealth of evidence all dates from the years of Lowry's celebrity after the mid-1950s. By this time he claimed (falsely) to have ceased painting his characteristic mill scenes and, as he grew increasingly consciousof his status as a media celebrity, the photo opportunities were carefully stage-managed.

In reality few individuals guarded their privacy as closely as Lowry, who was far from being the "simple man" he claimed to be. He gave evasive replies to the questions about his painting methods posed by curators or well-meaning friends (who, sadly, were not usually themselves artists), and varied the account in its crucial details. Furthermore, unlike an artist such as Cézanne, Lowry left few, if any, unfinished works. Consequently, very little is known about his working procedures - especially the manner in which he tackled the iconic industrial scenes of the 1920s and 1930s.

Left *Lowry at work in his studio in the 1960s.*

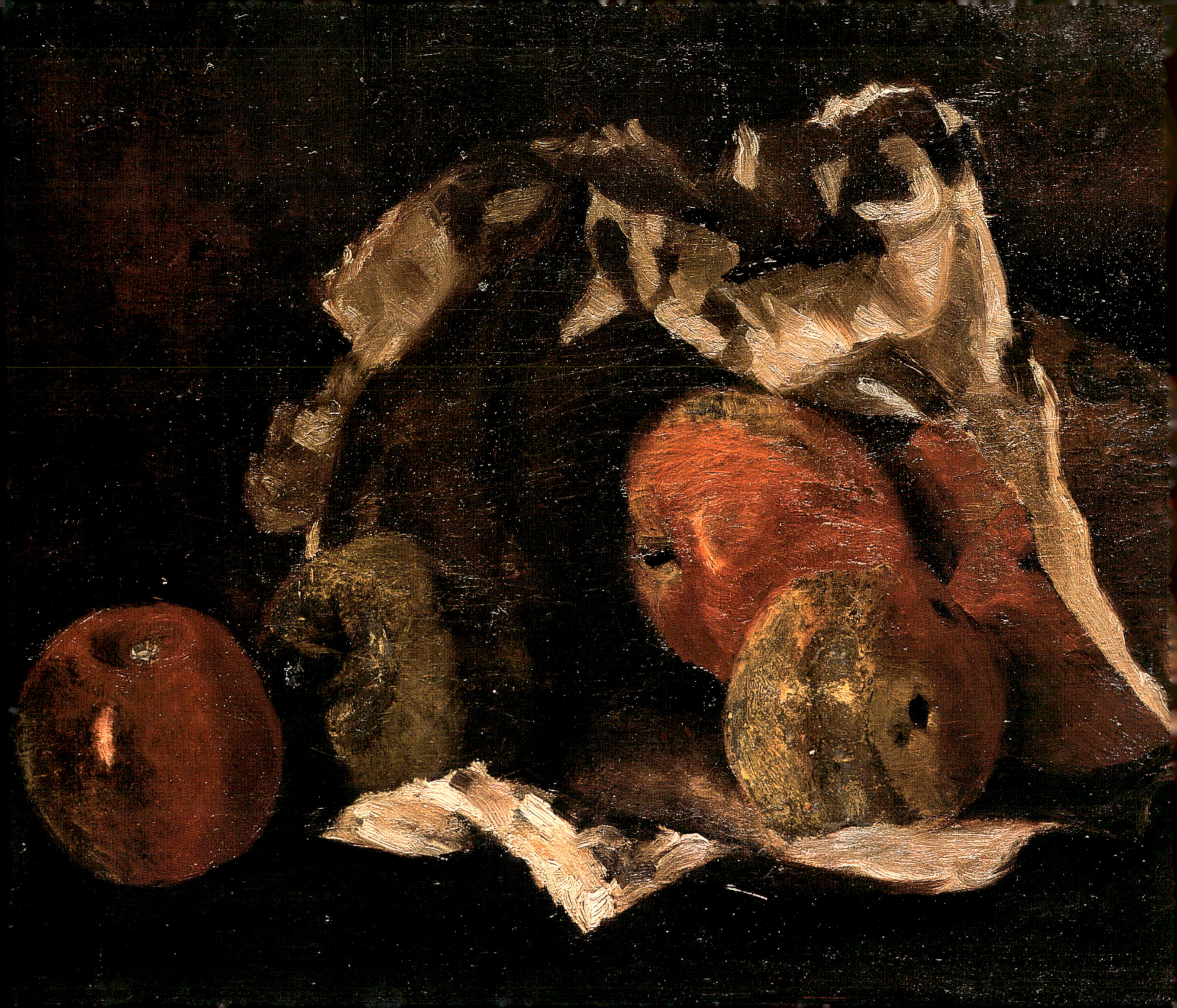

Left *Still Life with Apples, 1906.* *An early painting executed using mainly earth colours plus vermilion.*

Below *Male Nude from the Antique, c 1911.* *Lowry produced innumerable such studies in art school. As well as an HB he used softer pencils such as 5B and 6B.*

LOWRY'S TRAINING

During many years spent as a student in evening art classes Lowry received a training that was rigorously academic and traditional. There was no place for free expression. Whether he owned any books specifically on painting methods and materials [1] is not known but his studies began in the freehand drawing class followed by long hours spent making careful tonal drawings of plaster casts of classical statuary. Later he progressed to drawing from the clothed figure and the nude model in the life class. Though never professing to be in any way gifted, he always emphasised the importance of life drawing as a discipline:

"I did the life drawing for twelve solid years as well as I could, and that, I think, is the foundation of painting. I don't think you can teach painting, because everybody's colour sense is different. But drawing: the model's there, and you either get it right or wrong. There's no question of that. If you can draw the life you can draw anything." [2]

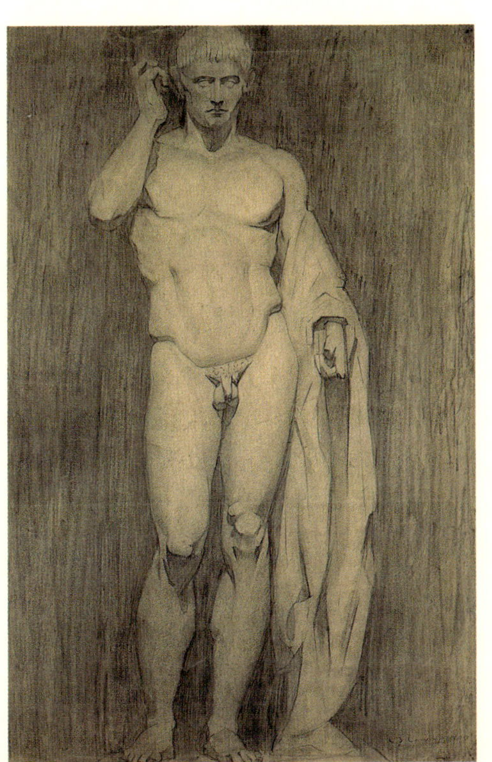

The drawings he produced were primarily tonal studies. He favoured either chalk or soft graphite pencils and used his fingers or an instrument known as a stump to blend the edges and smooth the tones. In this way he developed an ability to judge the most subtle nuances of shade that was crucially important when he later came to produce his oil paintings based on his characteristic white ground.

As early as 1903, however, Lowry had enrolled as a student for two evenings a week in the painting classes run by Reginald Barber, the Vice President of the Manchester Academy, where, he maintained, he painted "only heads". [3] He seemingly continued to attend for many years but, as if this was not enough, he also studied painting from 1907 to 1915 with an artist in Rusholme named William Fitz. Fitz set him to painting "one or two still lives" [4] but mostly more heads. Of these, Lowry said, only one survived. What he had done was re-use the canvases doubtless appreciating the extra "tooth" provided by the underlying painting. Although he informed Frank Mullineux that he had only done this "between 1910 and 1920", he evidently carried on with the practice throughout the 1930s and into the 1940s. Both *Man With Red Eyes, 1938* and *Blitzed Site, 1942* are painted on top of art school studies.

Apart from the *Portrait of Mr Brookes Heywood,* Lowry's earliest surviving paintings are simple still-life arrangements. These, too, helped develop his sense of tone, for careful attention has been paid to the disposition of light and shade ("chiaroscuro").

They are sombre works mainly painted using earth pigments such as umbers, ochres and siennas. Similarly, for the flesh tones in his *Portrait of the Artist's Mother* dating from a few years later, we may speculate that he used burnt sienna, flake white, yellow ochre and perhaps a little vermilion. These early paintings are also heavily varnished but he did not wish his later "white ground images" to be varnished. To protect them he merely wanted them to be put in glazed frames. Unfortunately gallery owners or collectors either ignored his wishes or were unaware of his preference. They often applied a layer of glossy natural resin varnish that has yellowed with time as can be seen in *Discord, 1943,* in the Lowry Collection.

He probably used mainly earth pigments for his first industrial paintings but, supposedly as a reaction to criticism of their low, indistinct tone by Bernard D Taylor, his teacher at Salford School of Art and the art critic of the *Manchester Guardian,* Lowry hit on the wilfully contrary idea of painting some figures against a pure white background. With such a stark image he returned to Taylor who praised the result. Whether Taylor ever corroborated this story is not known. Nor do we know which painting Lowry allegedly showed him. [5]

BACKGROUND TO THE PAINTING

Coming from the Mill is dated 1930. It was shown at the Salon d'Automne in Paris in that year and later became the third oil painting by Lowry to be bought by Salford Art Gallery. [6]
It entered the collection in October 1941 and is now, arguably, his best-known painting. It is still in its original state with very few cracks. As it has never been varnished the colours retain a beautiful chalky bloom resembling that found on the surface of a grape. But *Coming from the Mill* is not a portrayal of a real place. Rather it is a composite landscape (or "dreamscape") made up of a number of individual motifs from a variety of sources. Lowry himself described it as "my most characteristic mill scene", leading one to suspect that, in a sense, he regarded it as his "manifesto". Certainly there is some internal evidence to suggest that he set about its creation with particular care and it illustrates all the varied range of brushwork and special effects of which he was capable including dabbing, stippling, rubbing and more regular smooth, even brushing as well as considerable scratching out of detail and above all, scumbling. (Scumbling is where a layer of opaque paint is brushed over a dry, or partially dry, underlayer so it is incompletely concealed. The broken quality of a scumbled stroke depends on many factors including the roughness of the underlying paint layer, the thickness and quantity of the fresh paint to be applied, the type and size of brush and especially the speed and degree of pressure with which the stroke is applied.)

Below *Whit Week Procession at Swinton, 1921. This detail shows Lowry painted this picture working almost entirely "wet in wet". Another painting may lie beneath it.*

Right *Coming from the Mill, pastel, c 1917-18. This pastel is only slightly larger than the later oil painting for which it served as the prototype. Its crumpled, rubbed, torn state indicates that it has been roughly handled but Lowry cannot have referred to it regularly - otherwise it would be covered in smudges of oil paint. He has used a limited number of pastels to produce what is essentially a tinted drawing.*

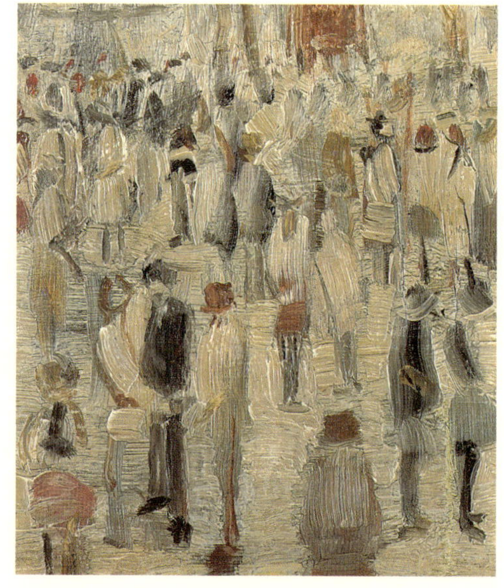

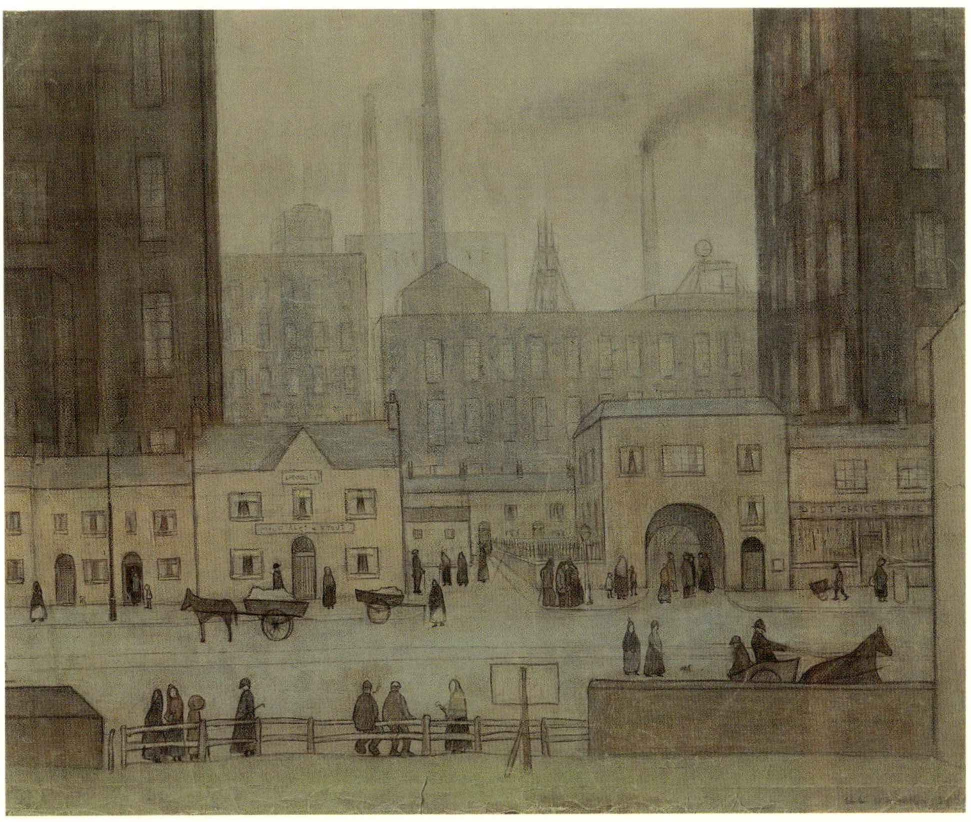

However it is very important to note that Lowry's painting technique constantly evolved. Even within a narrow period of time, he used more than one method. Particularly later, he painted more commonly "wet in wet" - where one colour is applied on top of another whilst it is still wet. He would finish such pictures in a relatively short space of time.

Furthermore, in one very important respect *Coming from the Mill* is not a "typical" Lowry for he had already produced an ambitious pastel around 1917 to 1918 which provided the basis for much of the composition. This was not his normal manner of working. Many of his pictures of single motifs were painted from less elaborate, preliminary sketches whilst other, later composite landscapes were developed on the canvas as he went along.

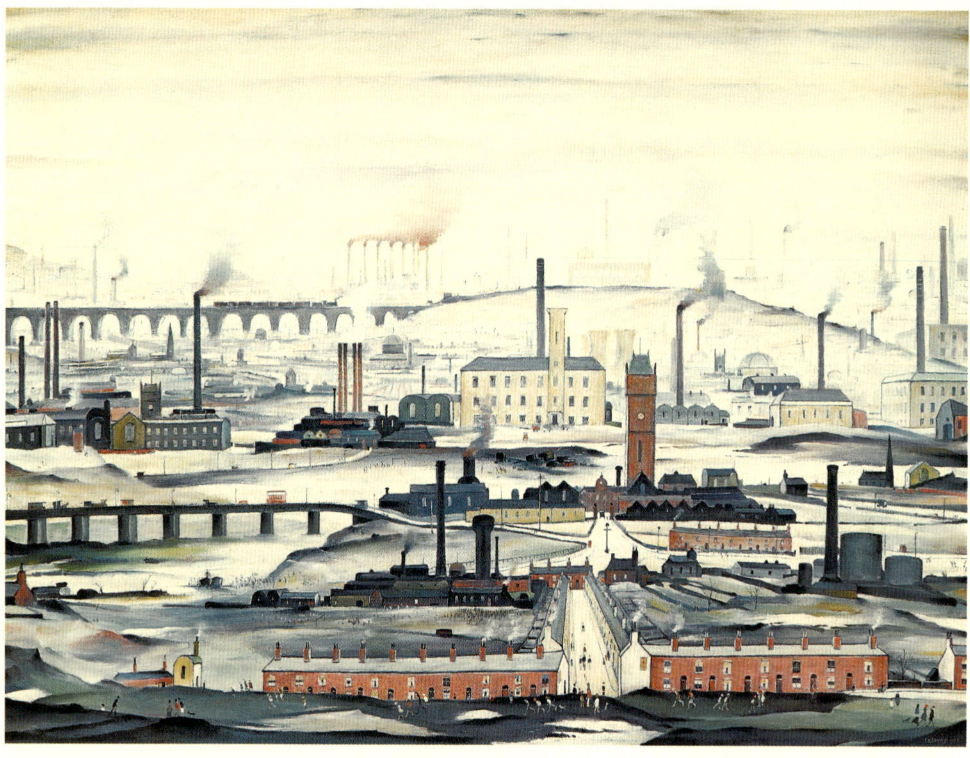

Left *Industrial Landscape, 1955.*

Right *Coming from the Mill, 1930.*
The back of the canvas showing Winsor and Newton's stamp.

"Very often I worked on the canvas entirely from memory. At other times I would make reasonably careful sketches on the backs of envelopes or scribbling paper like that. Then I would take that back inside to make a careful drawing and do the picture. But I liked in those days to do a picture entirely out of my mind's eye, straight on to the canvas. It was difficult to start, but you put something down, add to it, and suddenly you find you've put in some rather nice things and you're going along very well. It's like having to write an awkward letter. Once you've got a start to it you find it's not all that difficult after all. Oh, I liked that, to do a picture out of my head on the blank canvas. I think it gets nearest the truth, because there are no facts to hamper you, and you are setting down something that comes entirely from your own imagination." [7]

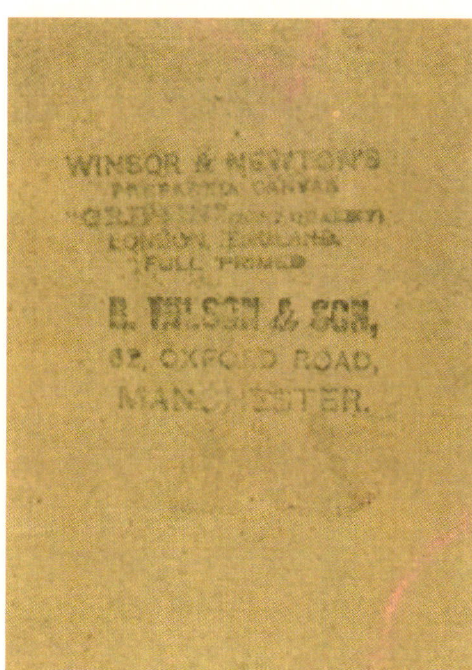

Similarly, writing specifically of his later *Industrial Landscape,* 1955, now in the Tate Gallery, he said: "When I started in on the plain canvas, I hadn't the slightest idea as to what sort of industrial scene would result. But by making a start by putting, say, a church or chimney near the middle this picture seemed to come bit by bit". [8] Such images were accordingly voyages of discovery through his own subconscious. With *Coming from the Mill* his approach was more premeditated. Nevertheless he introduced several changes as work progressed. Specifically he seems to have altered the colours of certain buildings several times and the unearthly, moonlit appearance of the worn pastel is quite unlike that of the related oil painting.

"You can't get weight in pastels. I could never get weight. And I wanted weight. Pastel is too fluid. Pastel is a thing you can play about with and you can't with oil." [9]

LOWRY'S MATERIALS

Lowry revelled in the closest possible physical involvement with his materials. Not only was he happy to dab and smear his brush on his garments but his application of paint to the canvas was immensely tactile involving not merely conventional brushes but rags, fingers and knives and a variety of sharp instruments which he used to carve into the paint layer. At the end of a painting session, his clothes would be spattered with the raw materials of his craft - just as a sculptor ends the day covered in marble or stone dust.

The Canvas

In a manner which contrasts strangely with his use of the finest quality oil colours, Lowry painted on virtually any surface that came readily to hand including earlier paintings, worm-eaten oak or pine wooden panels, hardboard, plywood (both sides) and pieces of scuffed cardboard.

He later concluded that he liked wood best [10] but, for *Coming from the Mill*, he chose a full primed "Griffin" canvas measuring 43.4 x 53.5 cm. This was manufactured by Winsor and Newton but purchased from B Wilson and Son, 62 Oxford Road, Manchester. Of the 29 varieties of canvas offered by Winsor and Newton in 1928 this was the company's best, most expensive canvas. It was woven from pure flax and was described as being suitable for "a subject with much careful detail; also for portraiture, where the visible texture of the materials painted upon, especially in the faces, is undesirable." [11] With the outbreak of war in 1939 its manufacture ceased and today the firm provides only three varieties of canvas. None is available in the size Lowry used for *Coming from the Mill.*

Lowry's Ground

Lowry had little or no interest in the aesthetic qualities offered by the different types of canvas or surface he used. Instead he aimed to obliterate the weave of the canvas or the grain of the wood with his own crusty white lead ground applied in several layers. This consisted of "Flake white in oil. Nothing else" [12] applied directly from the tube. Before he applied the second coat, he told Frank Mullineux, he might wait three months or a year and, occasionally, he might apply a third coat. Consequently, when he finally came to work on such a heavily textured surface it would feel like he was painting on rough stone. Later, however, mainly in the 1950s and 1960s, he sometimes painted on top of, or rather into, his white ground whilst it was still wet. What is often overlooked is that Lowry did not set all his images against a pure white background. (He preferred a Prussian blue tint, for example, for many of his large heads.) But a controlling white ambience is the unique hallmark of his developed style.

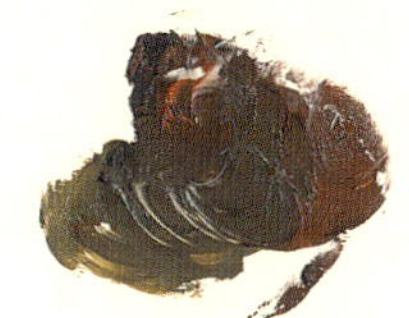

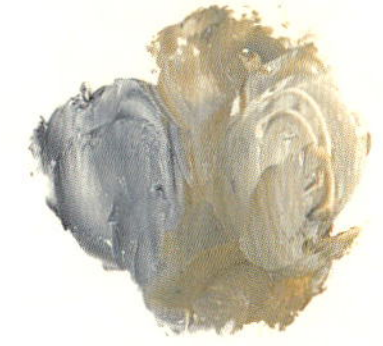

The effect it produces is certainly "unreal" yet it is not so far removed from actuality as is sometimes imagined. On an overcast day, after a shower of rain, light from a silvery white sky will be reflected equally from wet cobble stones, tar macadam and grey slate roofs. [13] As a consequence several of his paintings have a simplicity resembling that found in Japanese art.

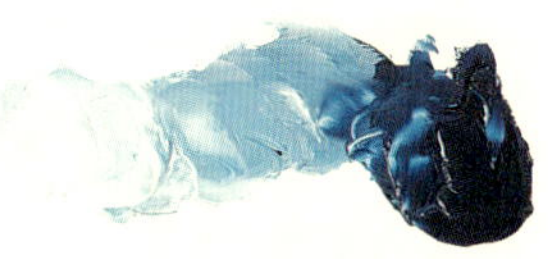

Lowry's Five Colours

As we have seen, Lowry's earliest paintings were produced using a rather different range of colours but he was insistent that he only ever used the five colours mentioned below. He never explained why, but the idea of using a very limited selection goes back to antiquity. Pliny the Elder describes how the celebrated Greek artist Apelles used only four colours but later writers on art suggested that five were more likely to have been used. Such academic speculation is to be found in *De arte graphica* by Charles Du Fresnoy, which Lowry owned, and in other books specifically on painting technique which he may have read as a student.

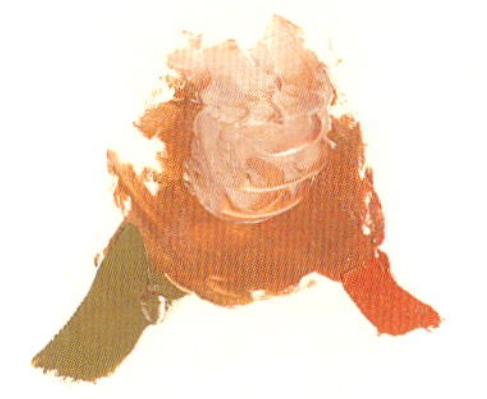

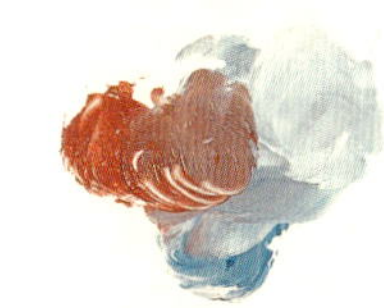

"I am a simple man, and I use simple materials : ivory black, vermilion, Prussian blue, yellow ochre, flake white - and no medium. That's all I've ever used for my painting. I like oils. Watercolours I've used only occasionally. They really don't suit me... dry too quickly. They're not flexible enough. I like a medium you can work into, over a period of time. That's about all there is to say on how I work." [14]

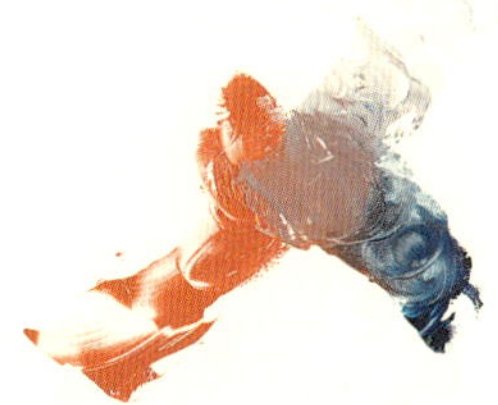

Left *Some mixtures of Lowry's five colours.*

Right *Detail from The Cripples, 1949. To paint the red scarf Lowry has used alizarin crimson.*

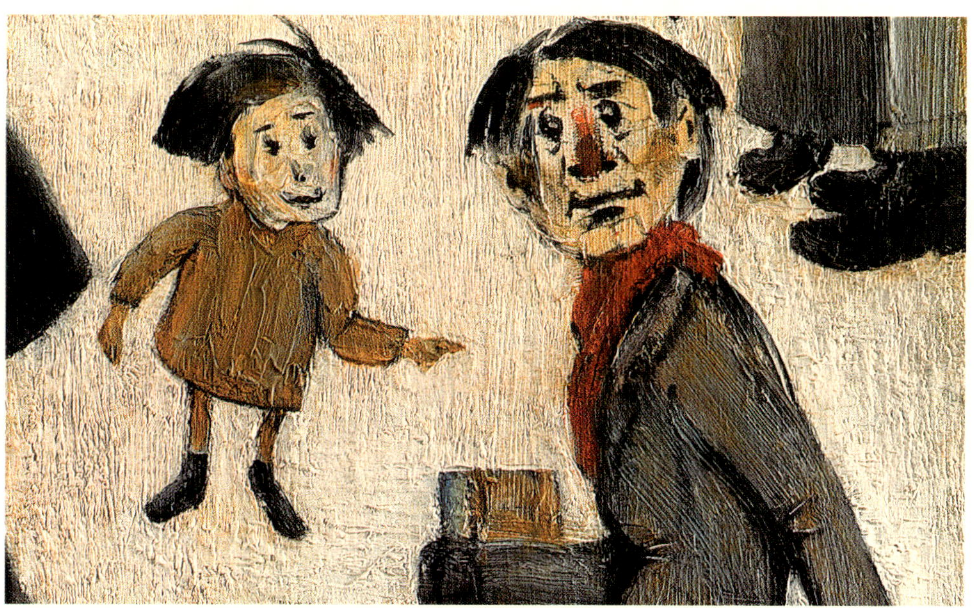

In Fitz's painting class, Lowry would almost certainly have been set the task of producing a picture using only black and white and one "less obvious" red, yellow and blue. [15] He chose three colours which provide a generally sombre range of hues which harmonise very satisfactorily with the appearance of the industrial environment in which he found his subject matter. However, visual examination and replication suggest that he occasionally used other colours. To paint *The Cripples* in 1949, for example, he must have used alizarin crimson in place of scarlet vermilion. A fairly wide range of muted hues can be achieved using mixtures of Lowry's five favourite pigments. Each pigment has its own history and distinctive handling qualities but some variety in the same pigment, manufactured by different suppliers, is to be expected. This could have helped to further extend the range of his palette if, for example, he did not confine himself solely to Winsor and Newton's materials. Vermilion can vary in hue, as can yellow ochre. (Different batches or sources - even the degree to which the pigment is ground - can affect the hue.) Price may also have had some bearing on Lowry's decision. Four of the five were amongst the cheapest, most common colours available during his lifetime and they remain so today. The exception is scarlet vermilion but, as Lowry was extremely frugal, he may occasionally have used a cheaper substitute.

Moreover, such an expensive colour may not always have been available from suppliers in Manchester - though presumably he also bought materials during his visits to London.

A further reason underlying his selection may have been that, with the exception of yellow ochre, the five colours are noteworthy for their covering power and tinting strength. One can argue that the potency of his colours, especially Prussian blue, echoes the "boldness" found in his drawings. Lowry mainly worked by artificial light in the evenings and Hugh Maitland thought initially that he had chosen the five colours "to facilitate painting by artificial light". In this there may be truth only insofar as Lowry would have grown familiar with virtually every mixture that was possible in accustomed artificial illumination. More colours would have increased the likelihood of the painting looking different in other lights.

Whites

Three types of white paint were available to Lowry as artists' oil colours manufactured by Winsor and Newton. Each has its advantages and disadvantages and very often small amounts of one pigment are added to another to produce a paint with satisfactory handling properties.

Titanium White (titanium dioxide)

Titanium White is the most brilliant of all the white pigments. Its covering power is twice that of white lead but for Lowry it possessed two distinct disadvantages. Although very durable it does not alter or mellow with time and, secondly, it is very slow to dry in oil. [16] Titanium White came into use as an artist's oil colour around 1920 - interestingly about the time that Lowry began painting on a white ground. Whether he used it then or only briefly in the 1950s (as he claimed) before reverting to white lead could be established by scientific examination but visual examination suggests that he used it for *The Funeral Party,* 1953.

White Lead (basic lead carbonate) and "The Drop"

Known in antiquity, Flake White (or White lead) has been described as "the most important pigment in the history of Western painting". [17] Though toxic if ingested, this did not prevent its use in 18th-century Europe as a cosmetic. White lead oil paint dries quickly to produce a hard crusty paint film with lots of "tooth". Equally importantly, it accelerates the drying times of other colours with which it is mixed. (Years of experience would have enabled Lowry to gauge this very accurately. Depending on thickness, colours mixed with Flake White would usually have dried sufficiently for him to do some further work on a picture 24 or 48 hours later.) Winsor and Newton manufactured two types of white lead but Lowry did not say

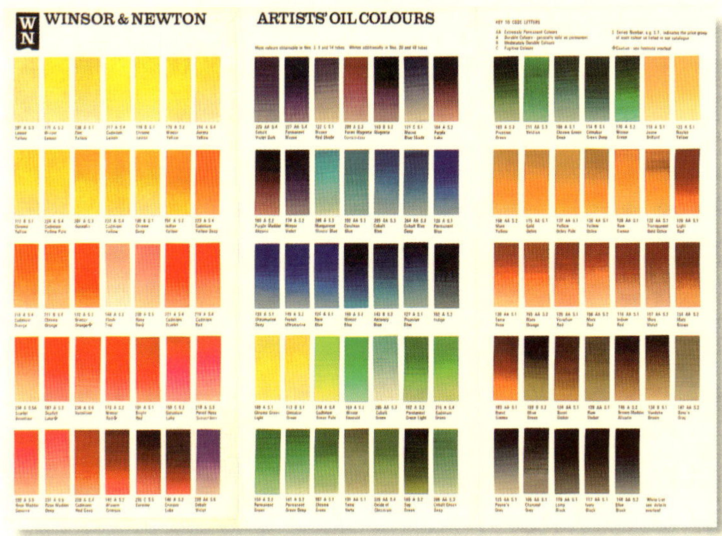

Right *A Winsor and Newton colour chart from the end of Lowry's lifetime showing the very wide range of artists' quality oil colours he could have used but largely chose to ignore.*

which he used. Flake White No. 1 is much stiffer and dries more rapidly than Flake White No.2. Each contains a small amount of zinc white (zinc oxide), the third white available to Lowry. The company explained how:

"*the addition of a little zinc oxide not only improves the consistency and general working properties of this pigment, but also conduces to the maintenance of its whiteness and enables it to give clearer tints with the colder colours. Artists who prefer to work with the pure basic carbonate of lead employed by the Old Masters should use Cremnitz White.*" [18]

Cremnitz White is whiter than ordinary Flake White so presumably Lowry did not use it. Instead, contradicting the claims made by the manufacturer, he professed to like the way Flake White "dropped", especially when compared to Titanium White. By this he meant the way the colour can change with time, which he claimed to be able to predict.

To explore this phenomenon further, Lowry affirmed that in 1924 he had painted a piece of board (or canvas - his account varied) with six coats of white lead paint which he then sealed and left for seven years. Upon opening it in 1931 - the year after he completed *Coming from the Mill* - he compared the aged paint film with a freshly applied coat of white lead. To his satisfaction he found that the older paint film had turned a creamy grey. Unfortunately he gave no more details of his experiment and did not say, for instance, whether he had kept the board in the dark. (It has been known for centuries that even the best grades of white lead paint turn yellow if kept from the light.) [19] Interestingly, the white background to *Coming from*

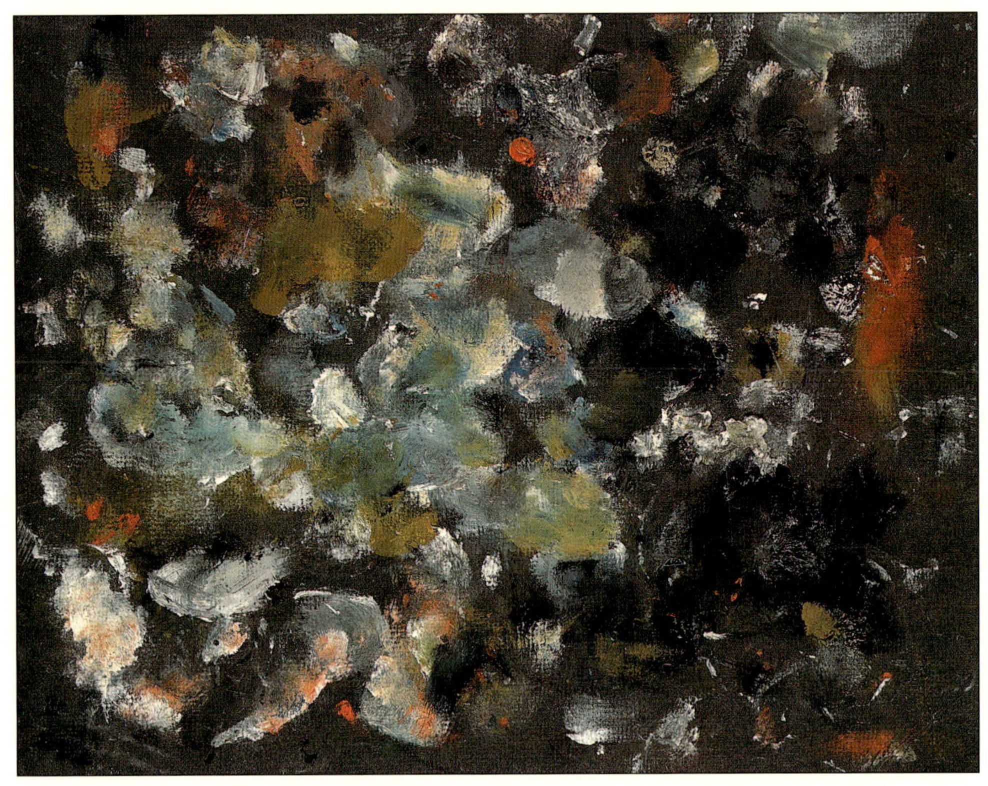

Left *Lowry mixed his paint on any surface that came to hand including scraps of card or artist's board. The status of this piece of dark brown card is unclear. There are no "pools" of his five colours and he may have used it mainly to clean his brushes of excess paint and mixed his colours elsewhere. Considering that he worked on a white ground one would have expected him to mix his colours on a white surface but over the years he grew skilled in judging the tonal and colour differences between paints mixed on one surface and applied to another.*

Below left *To paint the most detailed parts of his reconstruction of Coming from the Mill, Edwin Bowes rests his hand on a mahl stick, like Lowry, and he uses a small brush with a short handle designed mainly for painting in watercolour.*

Below right *A selection of materials used by Edwin Bowes to paint the reconstruction of Coming from the Mill.*

Below *To bolster his image as an artist of serious academic purpose (rather than a "Sunday painter") Lowry posed for photographers holding a traditional portrait painter's "studio" or "arm" palette which fits around the elbow. See the photograph on page 4.*

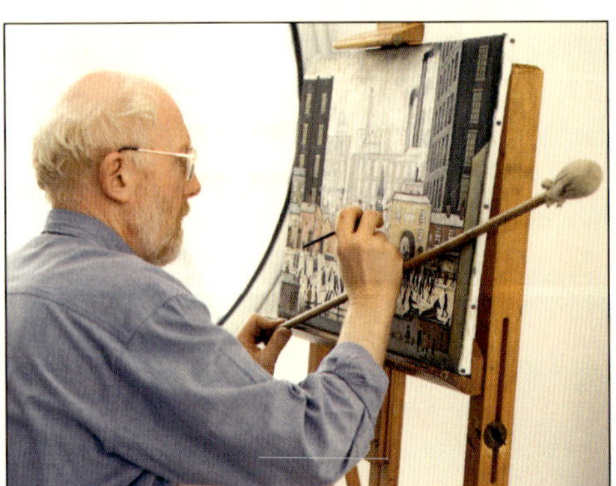

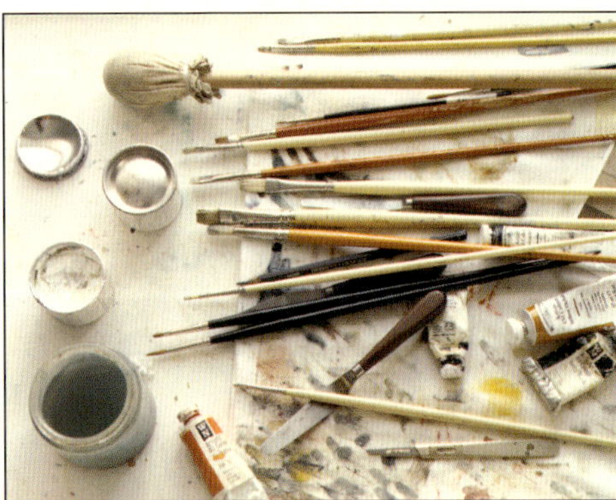

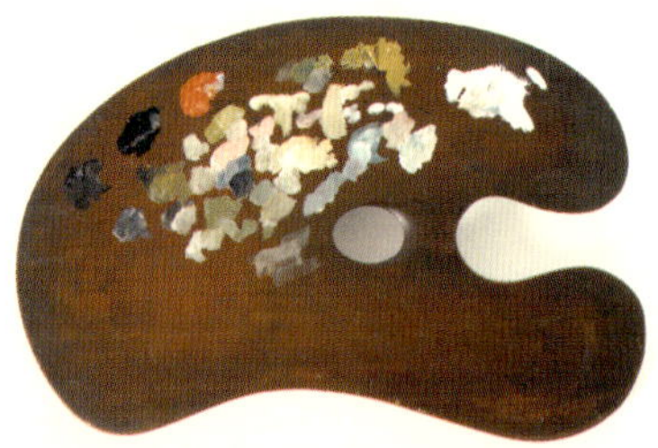

the Mill shows little evidence of Lowry's "drop". Though covered in a very thin layer of surface dirt the paint appears to have retained its chalky white purity.

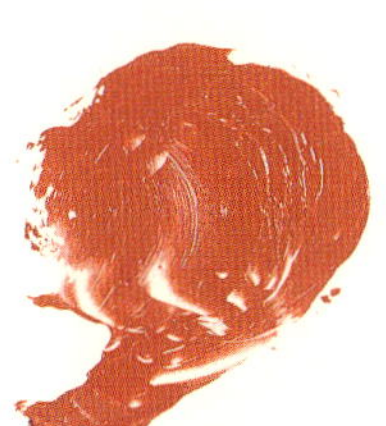

Vermilion (red mercuric sulphide)

Vermilion may be mined or manufactured artificially. In its natural state artists have used it since the earliest times. It has excellent body and hiding power but it is toxic. In watercolour it may blacken in direct sunlight but this rarely happens in oil. Its main disadvantages in oil are that it dries slowly and it tends to "settle out". Winsor and Newton offered vermilion in a wide variety of hues ranging from crimson through to orange. Scarlet vermilion, favoured by Lowry, is a slightly more orange variety than true vermilion. Both were expensive but pure vermilion was even more costly. Today vermilion has been all but replaced by Cadmium red.

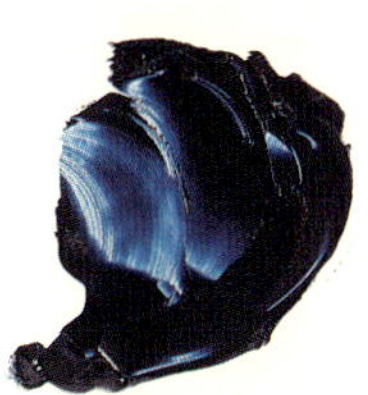

Prussian Blue (ferric ferrocyanide)

Prussian Blue is the first synthetic pigment with a known date of manufacture (the first decade of the 18th century). Originally made using bull's blood, it looks almost black when squeezed from the tube but really it is a deep greenish blue. Although transparent its tinting strength is so very high that 1 part "will render 640 parts of white lead perceptibly blue" [20]. It dries rapidly in oil and is a stable colour.

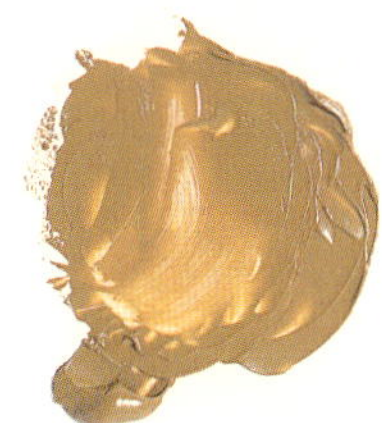

Yellow Ochre (iron oxide)

As a natural earth, yellow ochre occurs all over the world. Used by cave artists, it exists in a great many shades and degrees of transparency. The best varieties are absolutely permanent, opaque, non-toxic and cheap. Ochres are compatible with all other pigments but, since Lowry's time, more uniform artificial iron oxide ("mars") colours have partly replaced them.

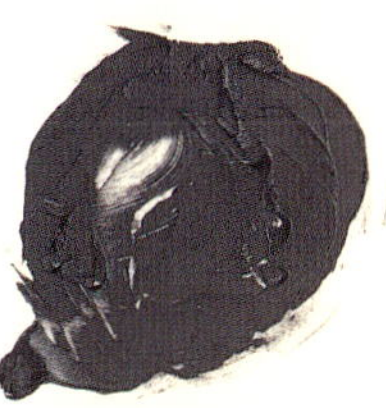

Ivory Black

Ivory Black, made by Winsor and Newton by "charring ivory", [21] was the most powerful, and quickest drying, of several black pigments available to Lowry. (Others included lamp, bone and vine black.) Ivory Black has a slightly bluish tinge but in the last sixty years little waste ivory has been available. The term is now commonly used for a black made from animal bones (bone black).

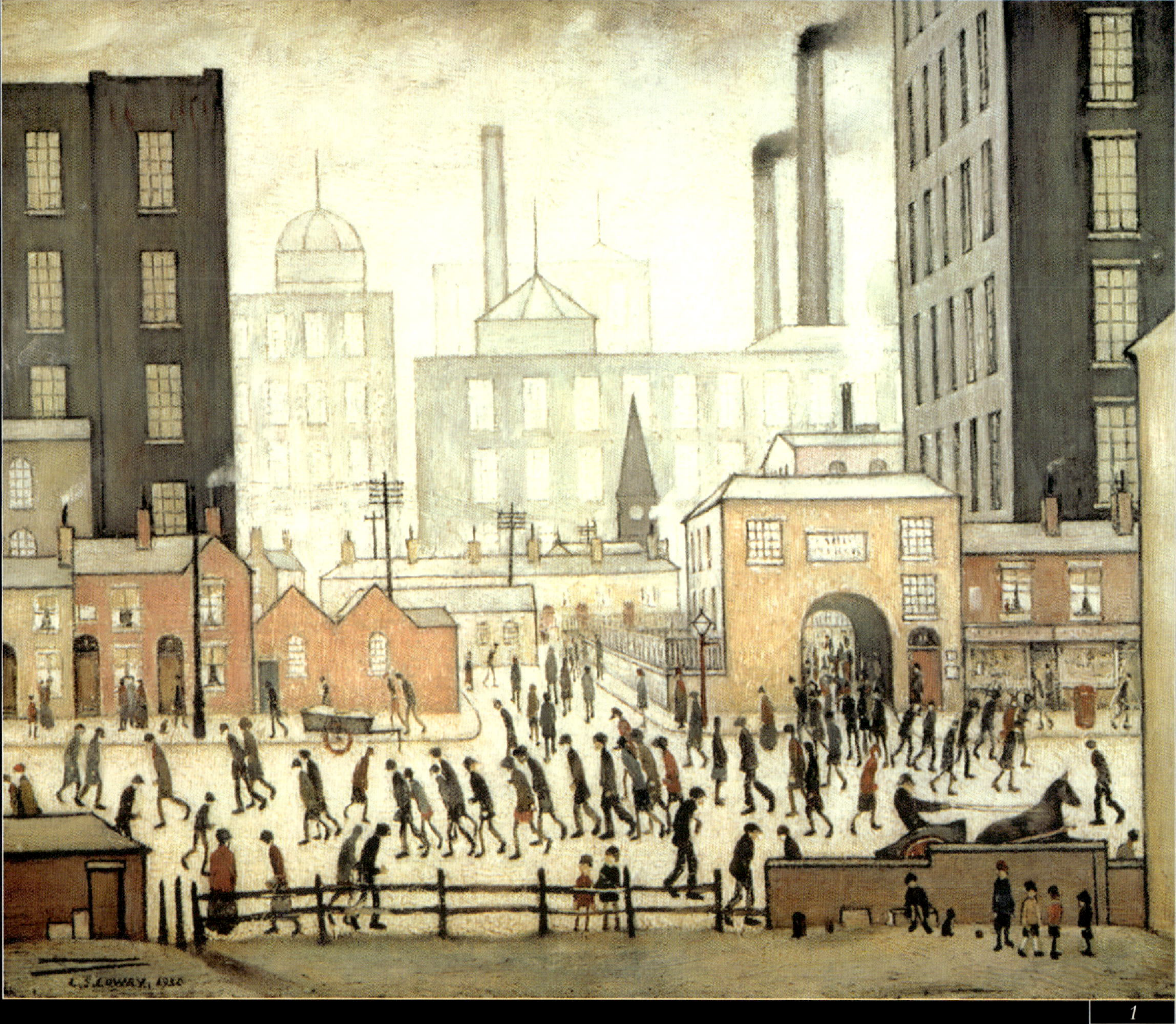

1

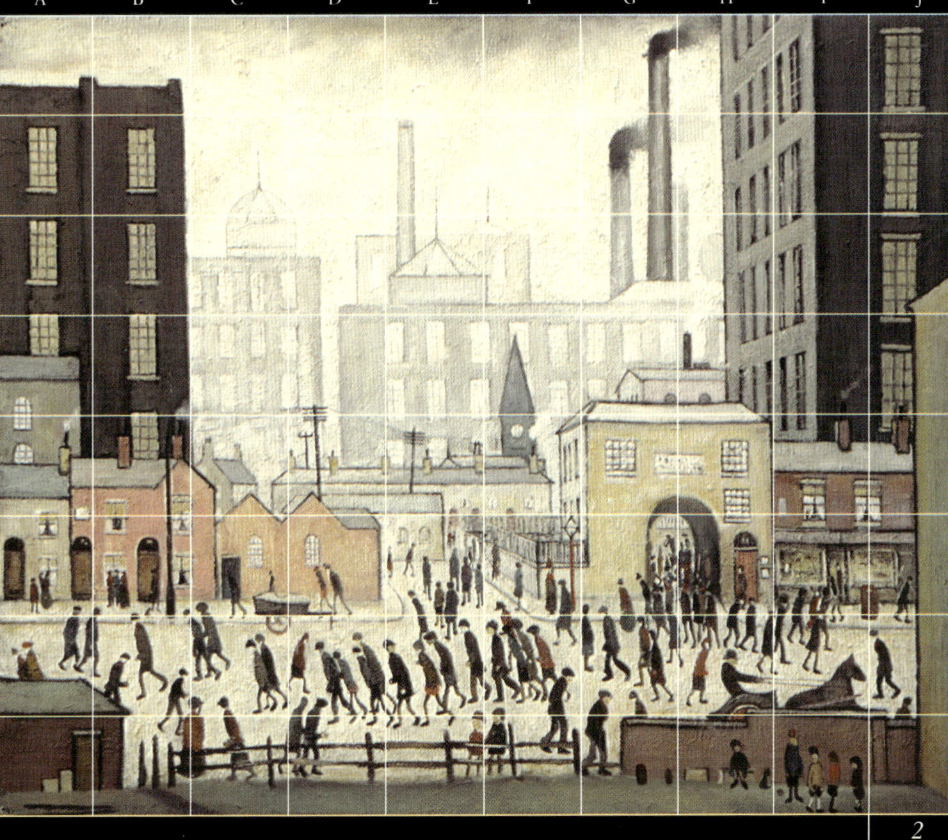

2

1 *Coming from the Mill, 1930, by L. S. Lowry, 43.4 x 53.5 cm.*

2 *Reconstruction of Coming from the Mill by Edwin Bowes, same size as original.*

Artists making their own reconstruction can take a reproduction of Lowry's painting and draw a grid over it. Then, if a proportionately larger grid is drawn on the board chosen for the painting, the position of the buildings and figures can be accurately copied onto it.

Colours: Artists will need two 21 ml tubes of Titanium white and 21 ml tubes of Prussian blue, vermilion hue, yellow ochre and ivory black. These can be mixed on disposable paper palettes and applied using a small number of hog and bristle brushes.

Brushes: One No 10 flat, one No 5 flat and one No 1 round, and a fine imitation sable brush with a good point, such as a No 3.

Other materials: A small knife with a sharp point would be useful for scratching out details, plus a rag and a palette knife.

The reconstruction (above) was initially painted from photographic reproductions and then from the original painting. The main disadvantage in working from a reproduction is that the image is two-dimensional whereas the original painting is a three-dimensional object in which the thickest paint stands out in high relief. Several changes have taken place in the manufacture and supply of artists' materials since Lowry painted his scene. For example, because of its toxicity, Flake white paint is less commonly used today and is no longer available in tubes. This replica was painted using materials as close as possible to those used by Lowry including Flake white, artists' oil colours, the finest hog and sable brushes and a very similar, high-quality linen canvas. However, a satisfactory copy can still be produced using "modern" materials such as hardboard in place of canvas. Lowry's textured ground can be imitated using acrylic modelling paste and Titanium white can be substituted for Flake white, although it is more chalky and takes a long time to dry.

The colour of the Winsor and Newton full-primed "Griffin" canvas bought by Lowry was a very pale bluish grey. This enabled him to see how thickly his application of his own white lead ground was covering the surface. He used multi-directional strokes and a large bristle brush - perhaps a No 10 or a No 12 flat brush.

Lowry claimed to wait for three months or even a year before applying a second coat and said he would occasionally put on a third coat. The first layer of White lead used for the reconstruction almost dried within 24 hours but was left for three days before a second layer was applied.

Flake White No 1, used for the reconstruction, is a very stiff paint. It does not flow readily. Lowry did not thin his colours with turpentine or add any extra oil or varnish to his paint. He only cleaned his brushes fully with turpentine at the end of the painting session though he would press out unwanted excess paint on to an old rag.

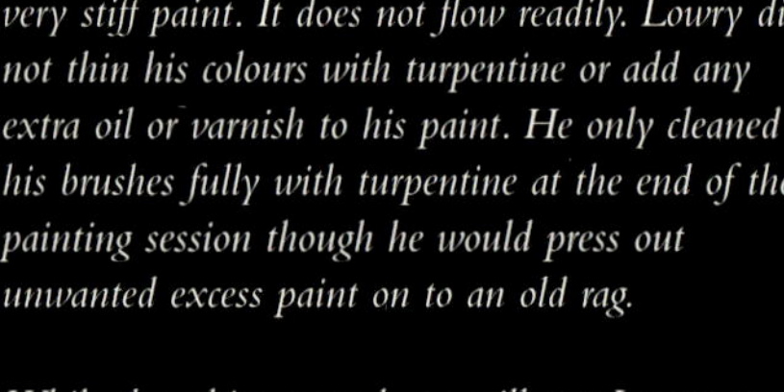

While the white ground was still wet Lowry may have experimented with positioning the main compositional features by "drawing" in the wet paint with his brush.

Once the ground layer was sufficiently dry Lowry probably sketched in the composition loosely in chalk, charcoal (as here) or pencil. He would not have worried about the purity of his colours being affected when fresh colour was applied on top of the lines.

Lowry used a measure to carefully mark the central point of the composition. "Balance" was a psychological imperative for Lowry. In this picture he achieves equilibrium through the repetition of key shapes and the skilful use of colour.

Charcoal drawing.

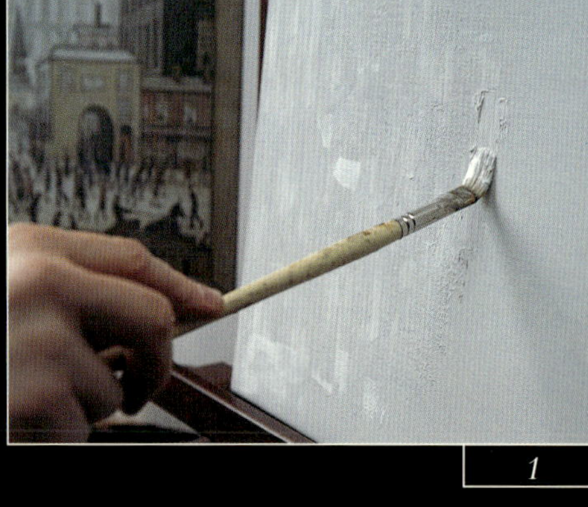
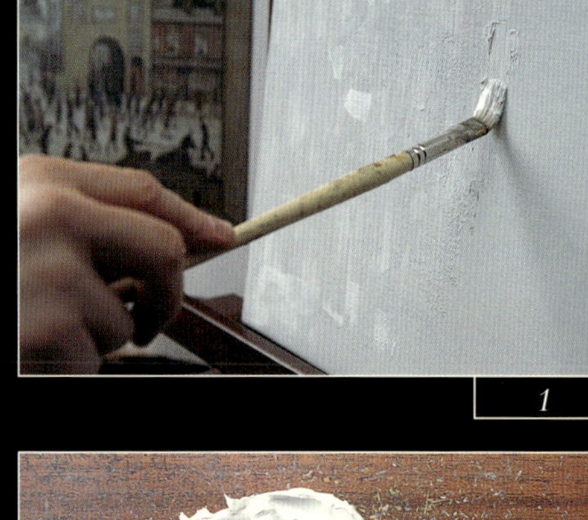

1

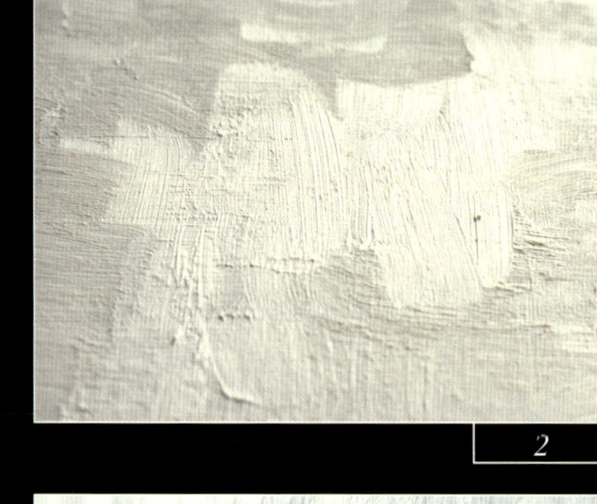

2

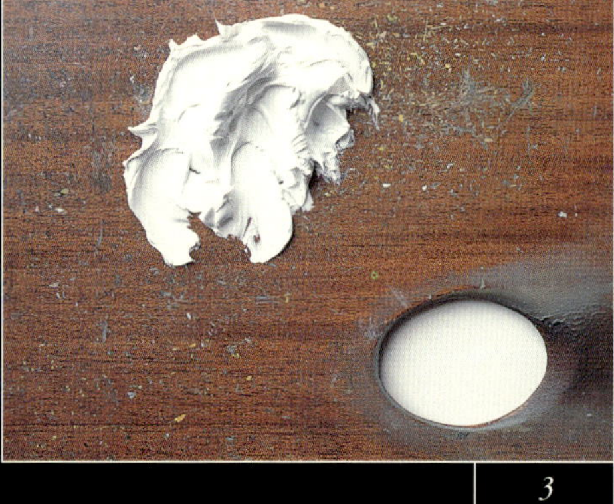

3

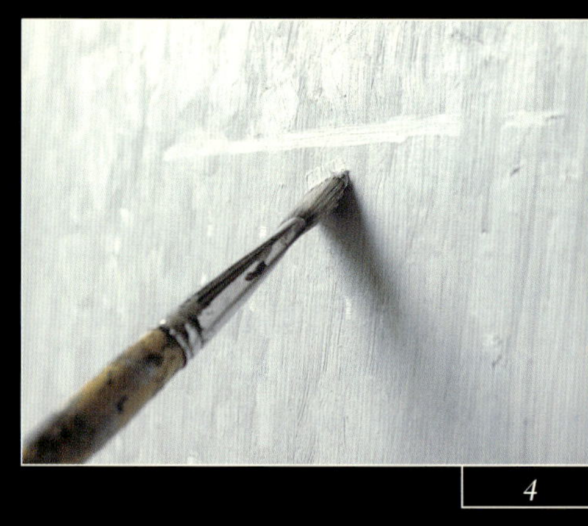

4

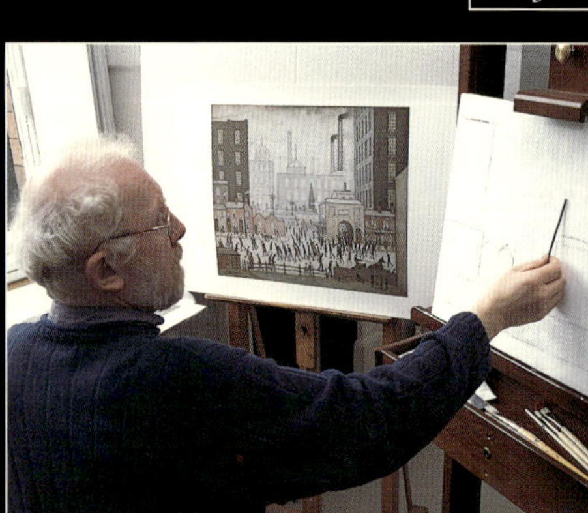

5

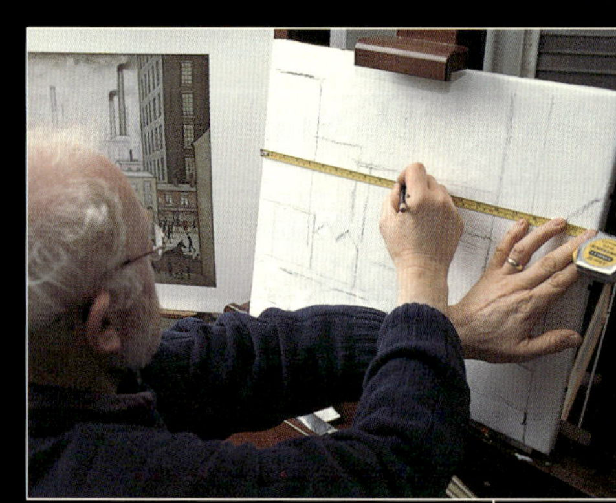

6

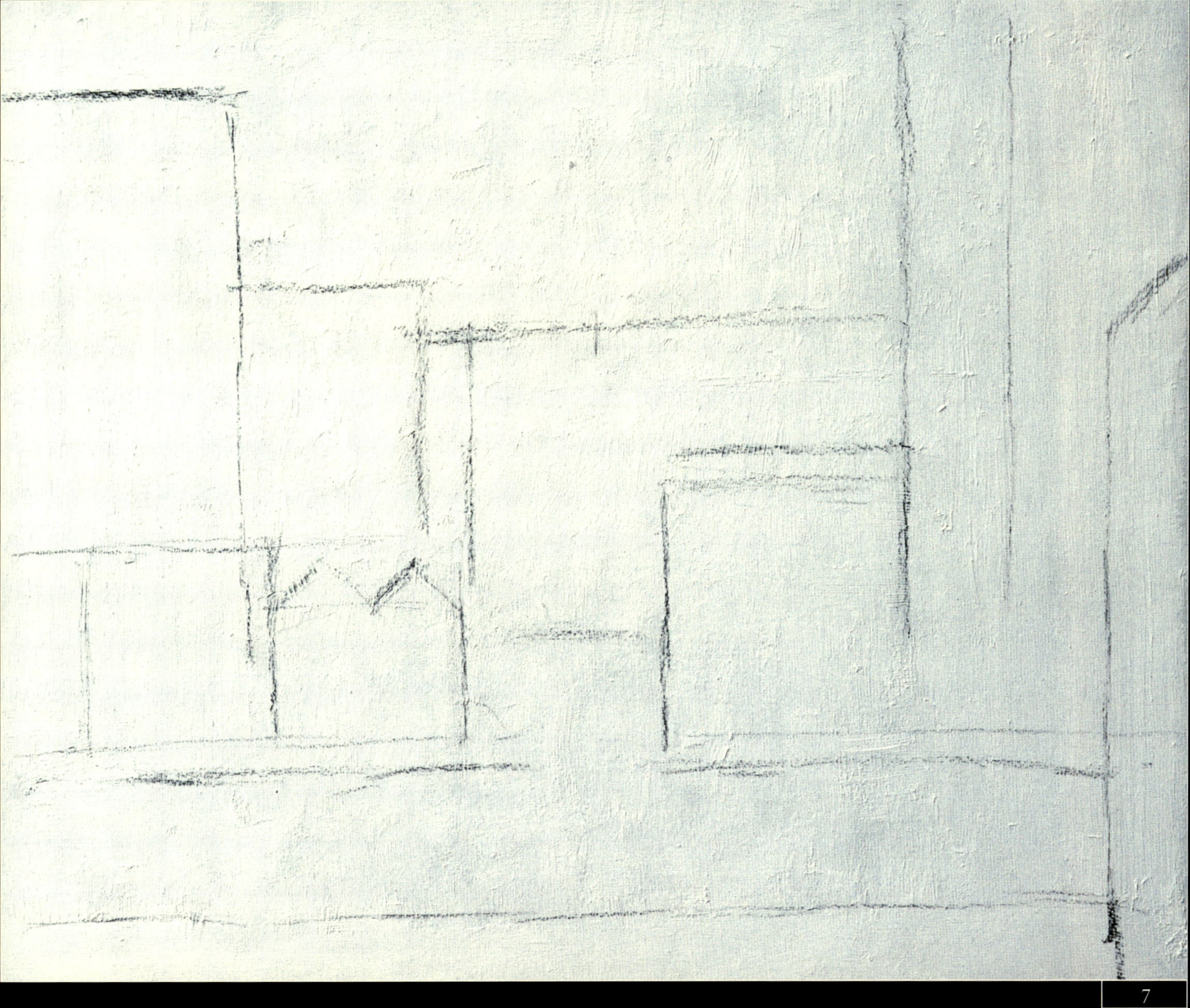

Using his pastel as a guide, Lowry loosely blocked in the main architectural elements as roughly painted tonal shapes using large well worn hog (bristle) brushes - perhaps a No 10 or No 12 flat.

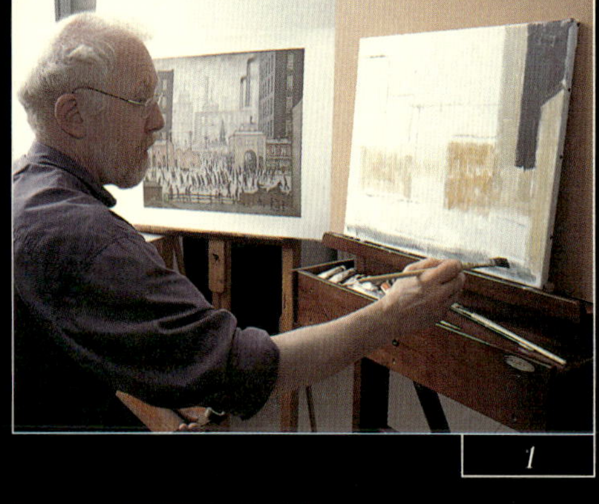

1

The stiff paint is dragged across the heavily textured white ground.

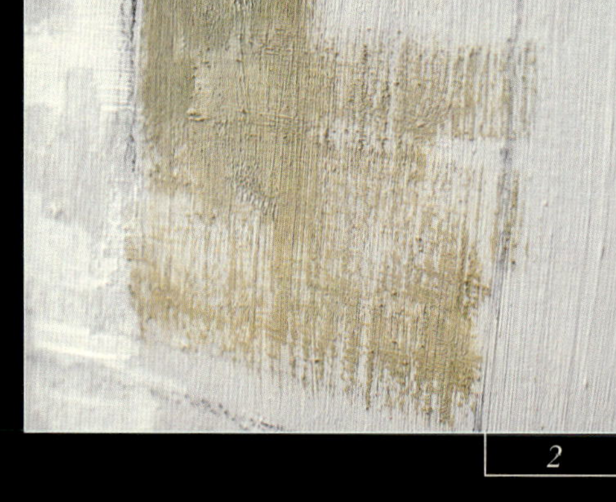

2

The left-hand mill has been blocked in to balance the one on the right. To paint the grey mill in the middle distance, a broad flat brush is used.

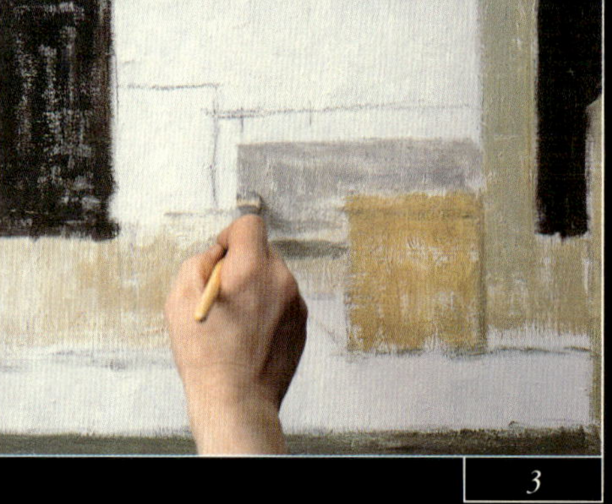

3

Lowry experimented with the colour of the different shapes and the balance between verticals and horizontals. A single chimney establishes a vertical element in the composition.

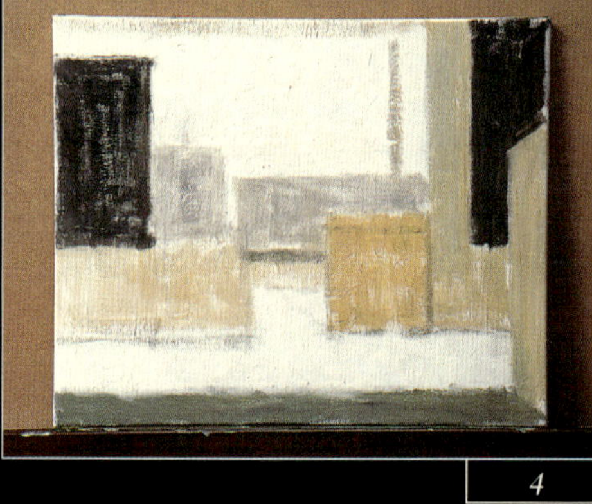

4

He would begin to tighten up the design - most likely by drawing on top of the dry paint using either charcoal, soft pencil or possibly black paint.

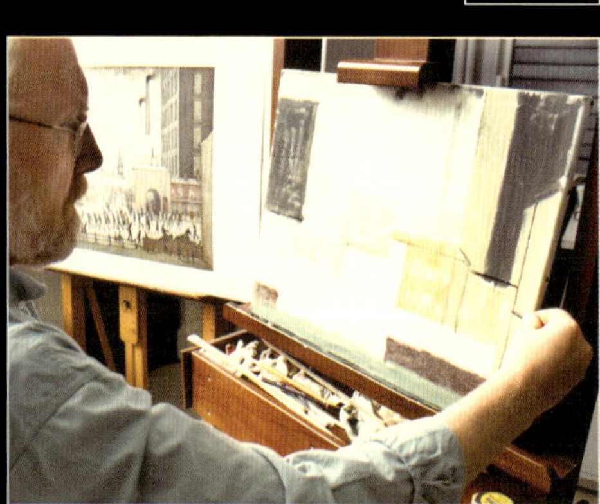

5

Use of the charcoal stick (detail).

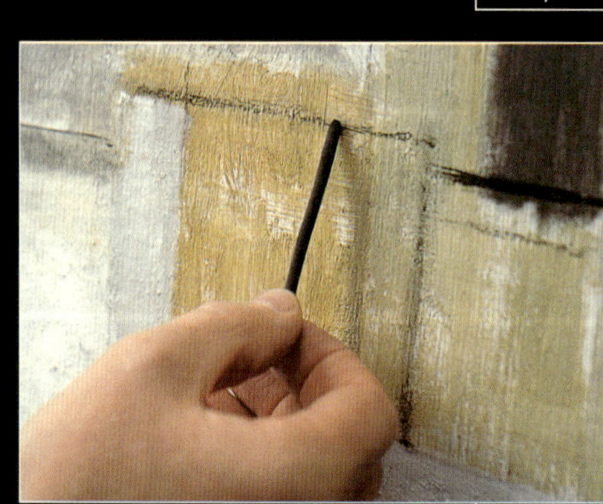

6

The painting is blocked in. Some guide-lines have been drawn in charcoal, pencil or paint but at this stage the composition is conceived as a series of two-dimensional shapes. He knew that much of what he applied at this stage would be modified later.

More architectural detail is introduced in the distance using a soft pencil. Along the top edge black paint is rapidly applied to suggest a pall of grey black soot. Found in many of Lowry's paintings, this dark strip also serves to contain the image within the rectangle of the canvas.

It is also possible to draw into the paint before it is completely dry with a very soft 6B pencil and a ruler.

To paint the pink houses behind the barrow Lowry scumbled a thin layer of pink over his blocked-in ochre. He seems to have used a rag to wipe off most of the excess pink. What remains is trapped in the deepest hollows of the ochre impasto.

With the application of additional scumbled colour the painting takes shape. At this stage Lowry intended that a building in the shadow of the tall mill on the left would be pink.

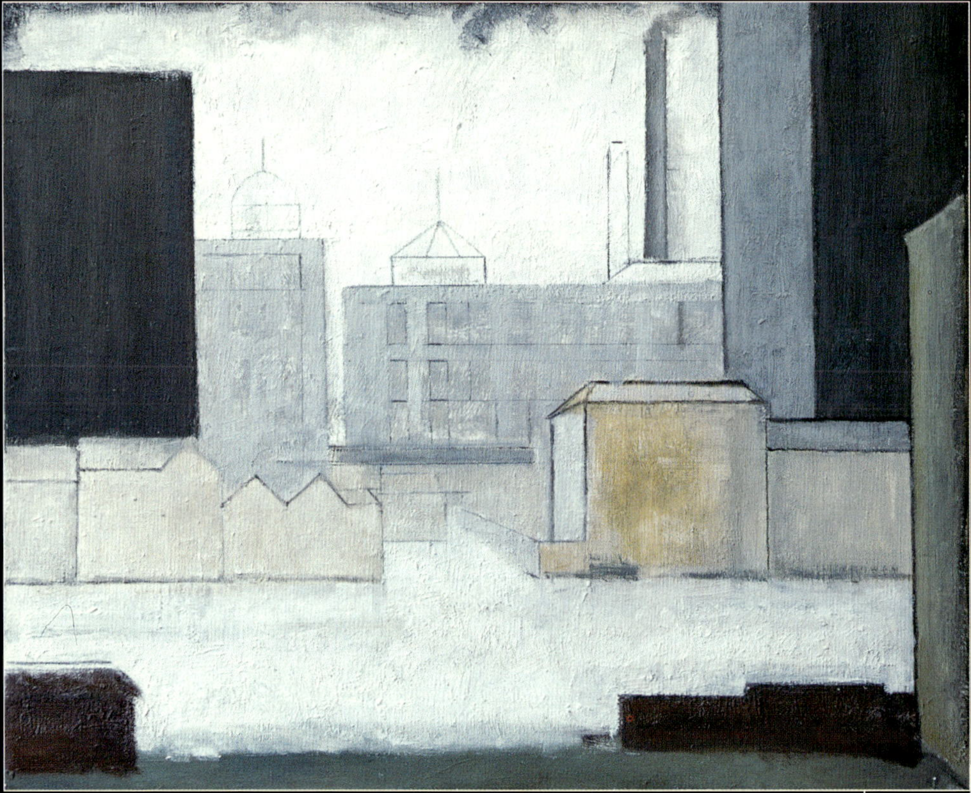

1

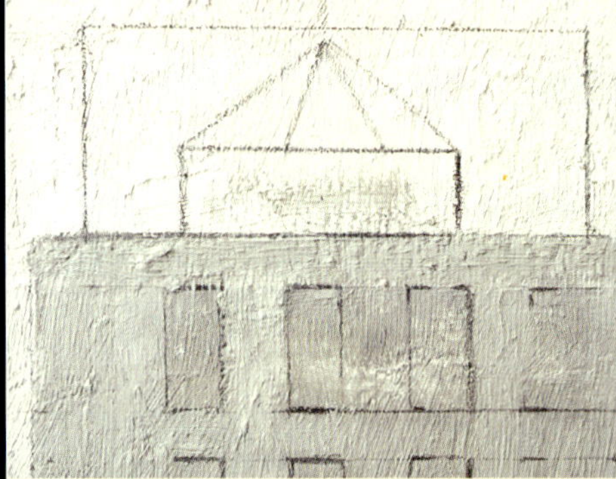

2

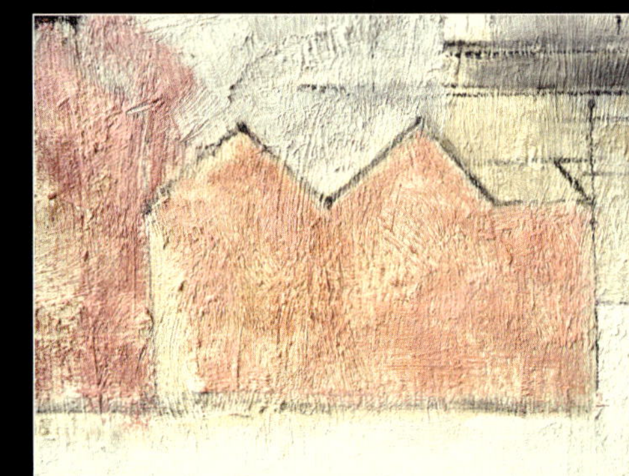

3

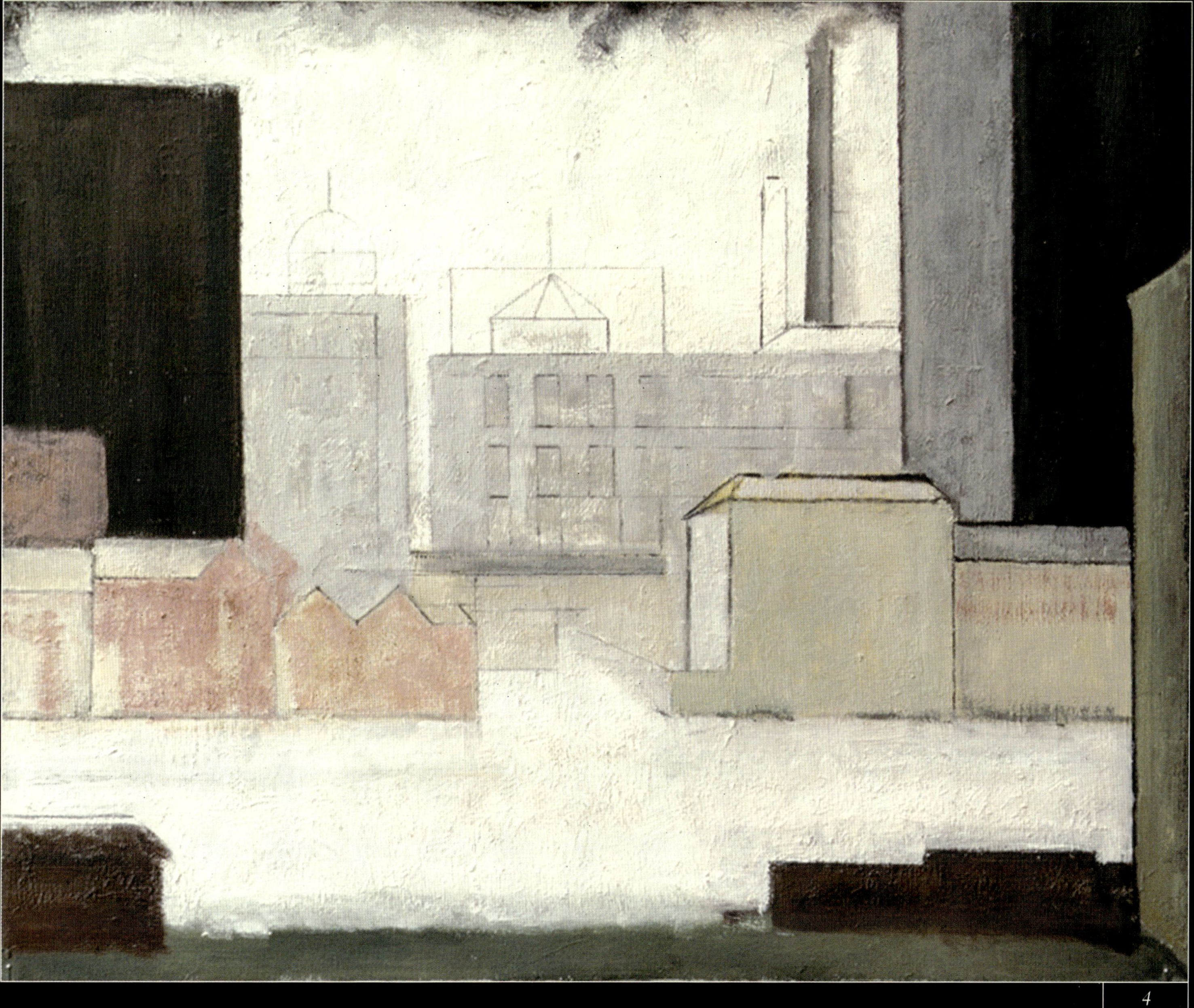

The next stage would be to paint in the blank shapes of windows, doors and other architectural features. Black paint is used to strengthen the outlines of buildings.

A No 5 long flat brush is used to paint some windows in the distant mill.

To paint the smoke billowing from the chimneys and blend other colours, Lowry probably used his fingers. This procedure is not recommended in case artists later inadvertently lick their fingers or bite their nails and ingest dangerous white lead paint.

A first attempt is made to replicate the shop front on the right by scratching through a thinly applied layer of black paint with a nail to reach the underlying ochre lay-in. In fact, Lowry painted this area quite differently by applying a thick layer of highly textured pale ochre. He then scumbled some black paint very thinly over it before scratching out some details.

Adding the low wall to the left of the main arch and windows to the receding wall of the mill on the right dramatically creates depth in the composition.

Lowry added more and more white paint to determine the edges of buildings so the sky is the thickest part of the painting and the distant grey mills exist at a shallower level. In raking light some parts of the picture resemble a sculpted relief.

Lowry would have put in some figures at the same time as he developed the buildings behind. We cannot tell the order in which he painted them but here a single individual is introduced onto an empty stage set to illustrate Lowry's point that "A street… without people… is as dead as mutton."

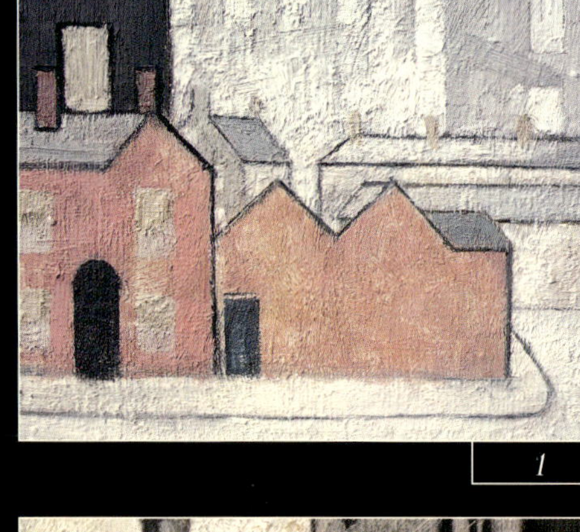

1

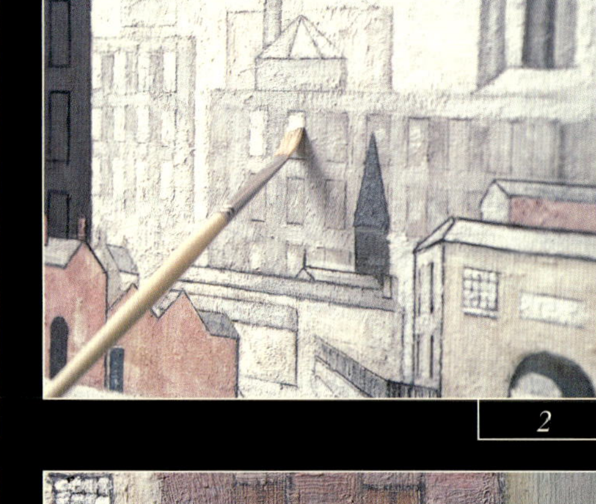

2

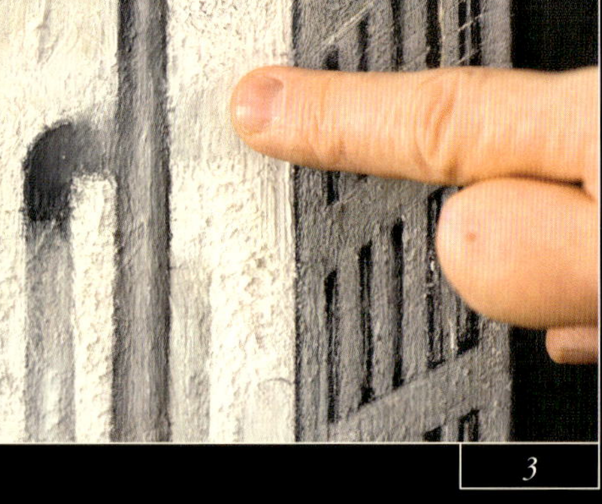

3

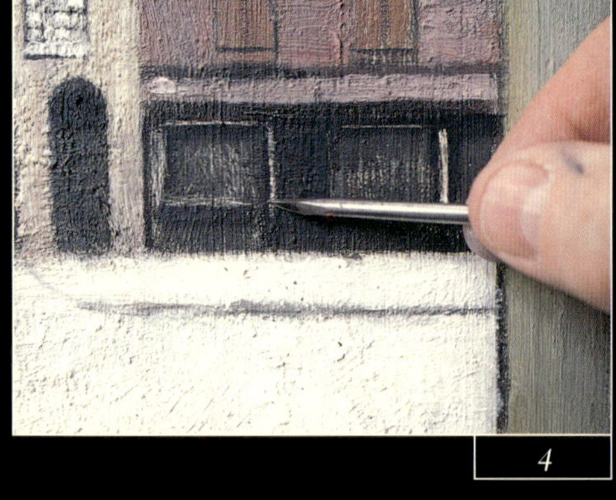

4

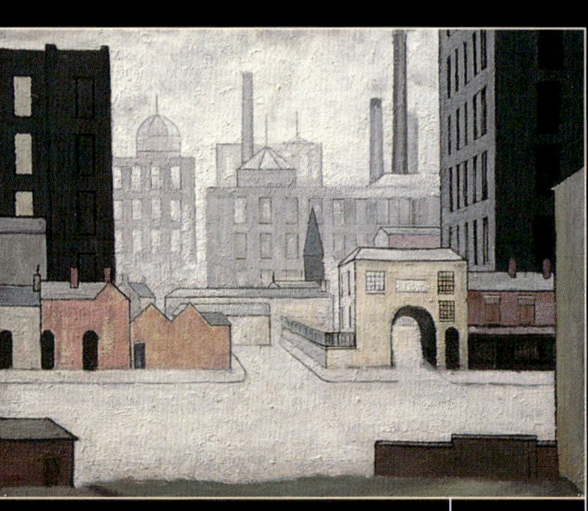

5

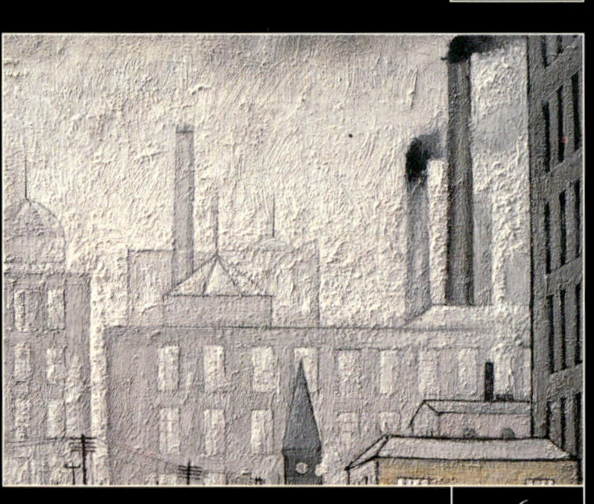

6

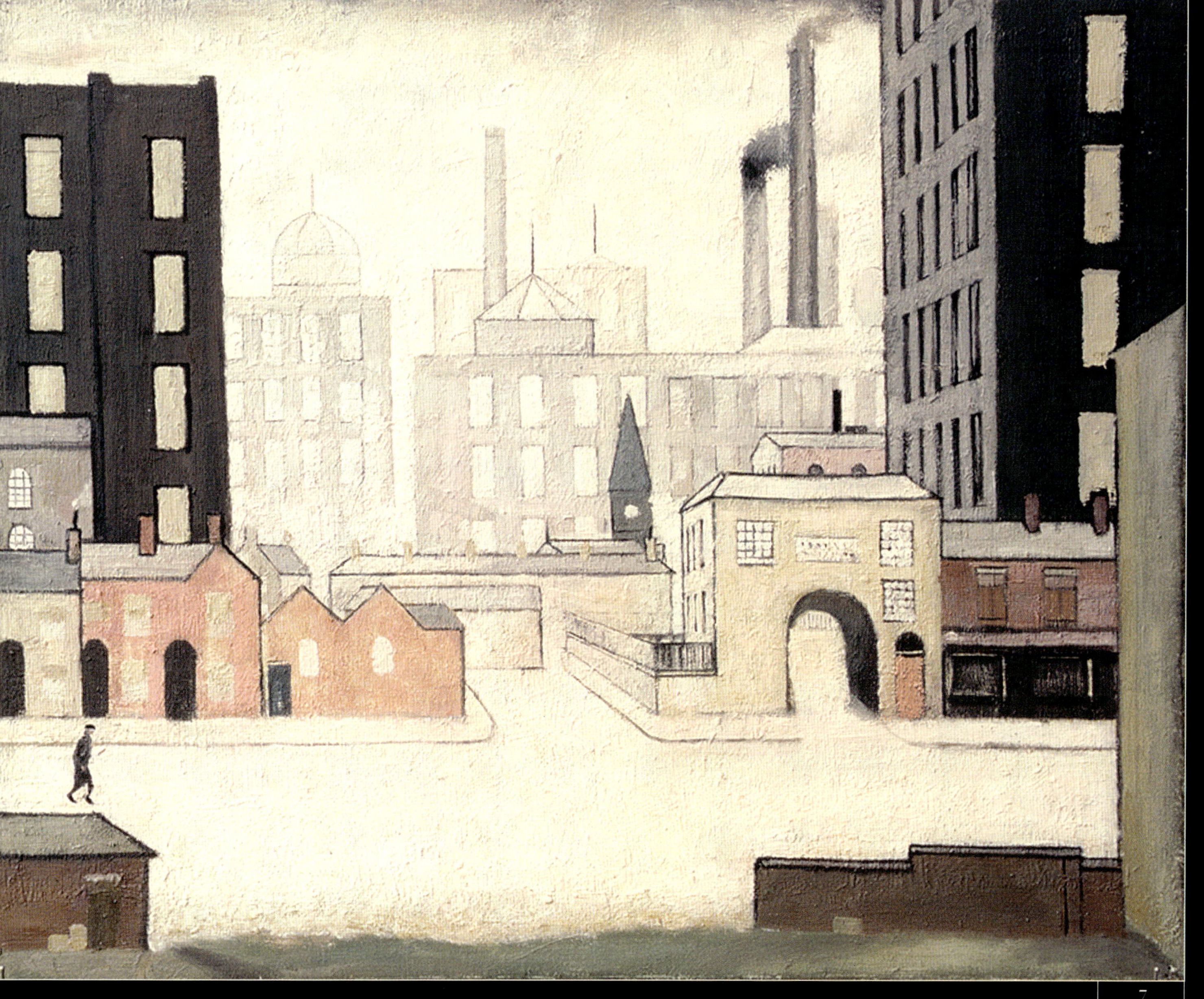

To paint the most detailed parts of the picture such as the window bars, Lowry would probably have used a No 5 round sable brush with a sharp clean point.

He mainly used brushes rather than a palette knife to mix his colours. Sometimes he would mix some colours on the painting itself, adding fresh quantities to combinations he had already applied such as the way in which a little red paint is mixed with the dark wall of the mill on the left of the picture. The danger in mixing paint on the canvas is that the crispness of the brushstroke can be lost and the paint can begin to look muddy and "dead".

To paint the tiniest figures in the distance Lowry applied his paint as the thinnest possible dry scumble with the very tip of a pointed No 5 round sable brush.

Oil painting brushes have long handles to permit the greatest versatility in their use. Lowry would rarely grip the brush by the metal ferrule for this would inhibit the free, expressive movement of his wrist. Instead, he held it close to the end or mid-way down the handle.

Lowry used a wide variety of brushes of varying size suited to particular tasks. A No 5 round bristle brush is best to paint the three arched doorways on the left of the painting. For the fence posts in the foreground, a No1 round bristle brush is recommended.

At most stages Lowry would use a penknife or the tip of a nail roughly 2mm thick to gouge out certain features.

More figures have been introduced and the shop front on the right has been repainted. Lowry didn't complete one area of his painting before moving on to another section. Instead he worked rapidly over the whole surface, adding one stroke here and another there.

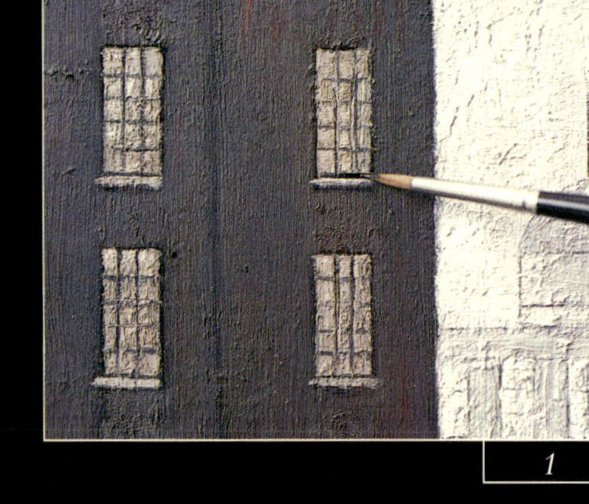

1

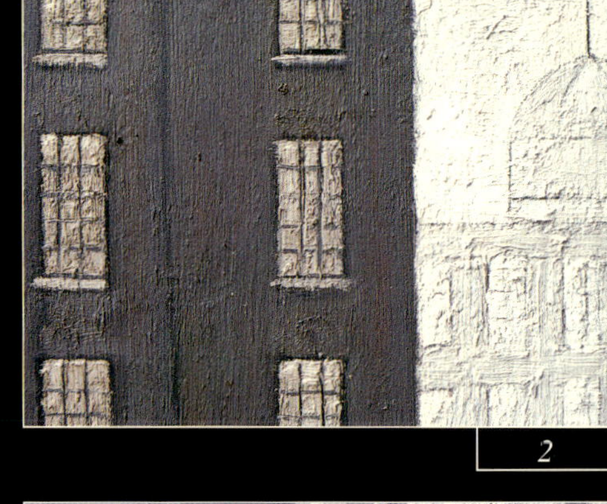

2

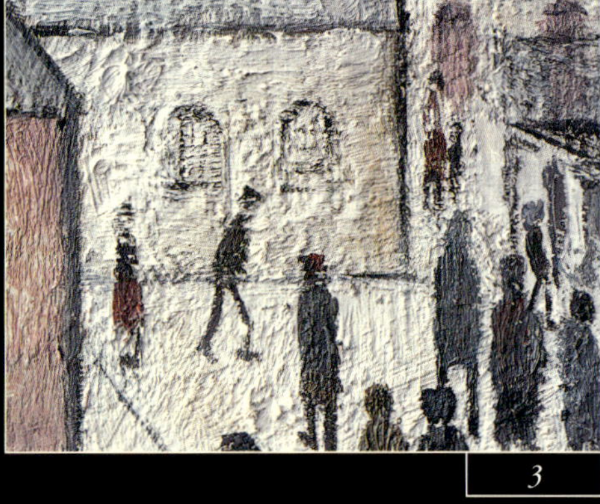

3

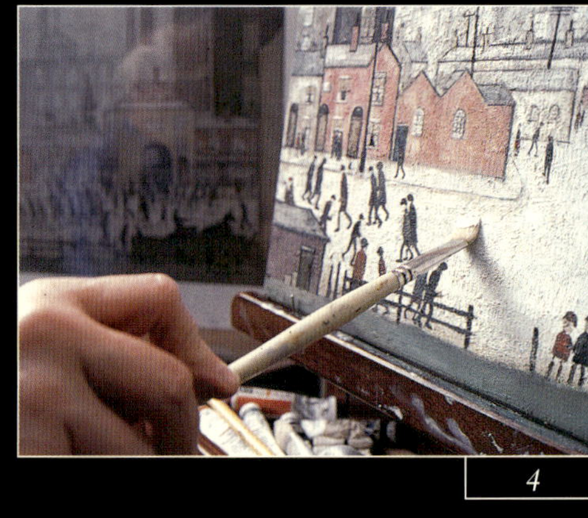

4

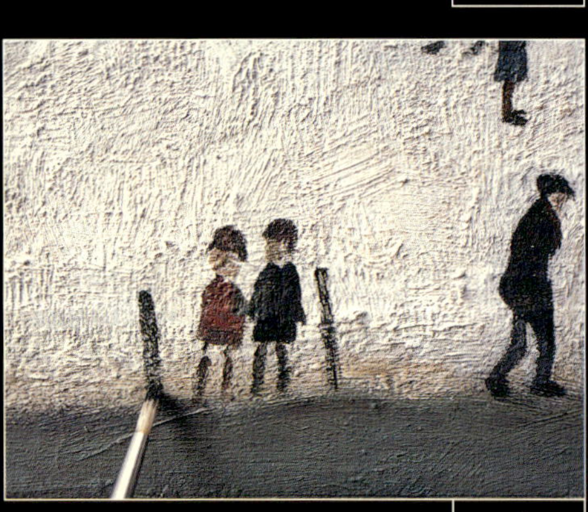

5

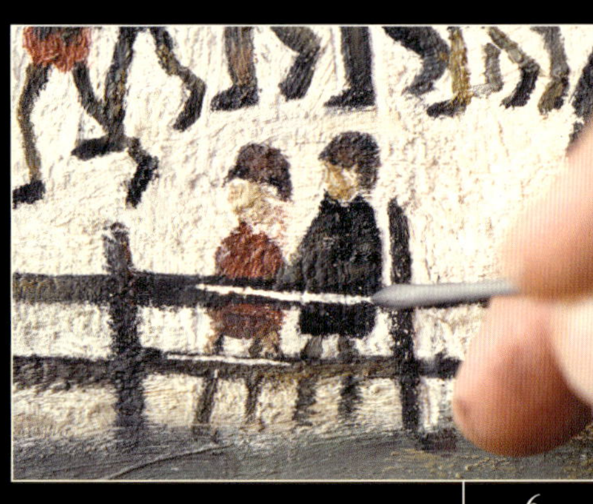

6

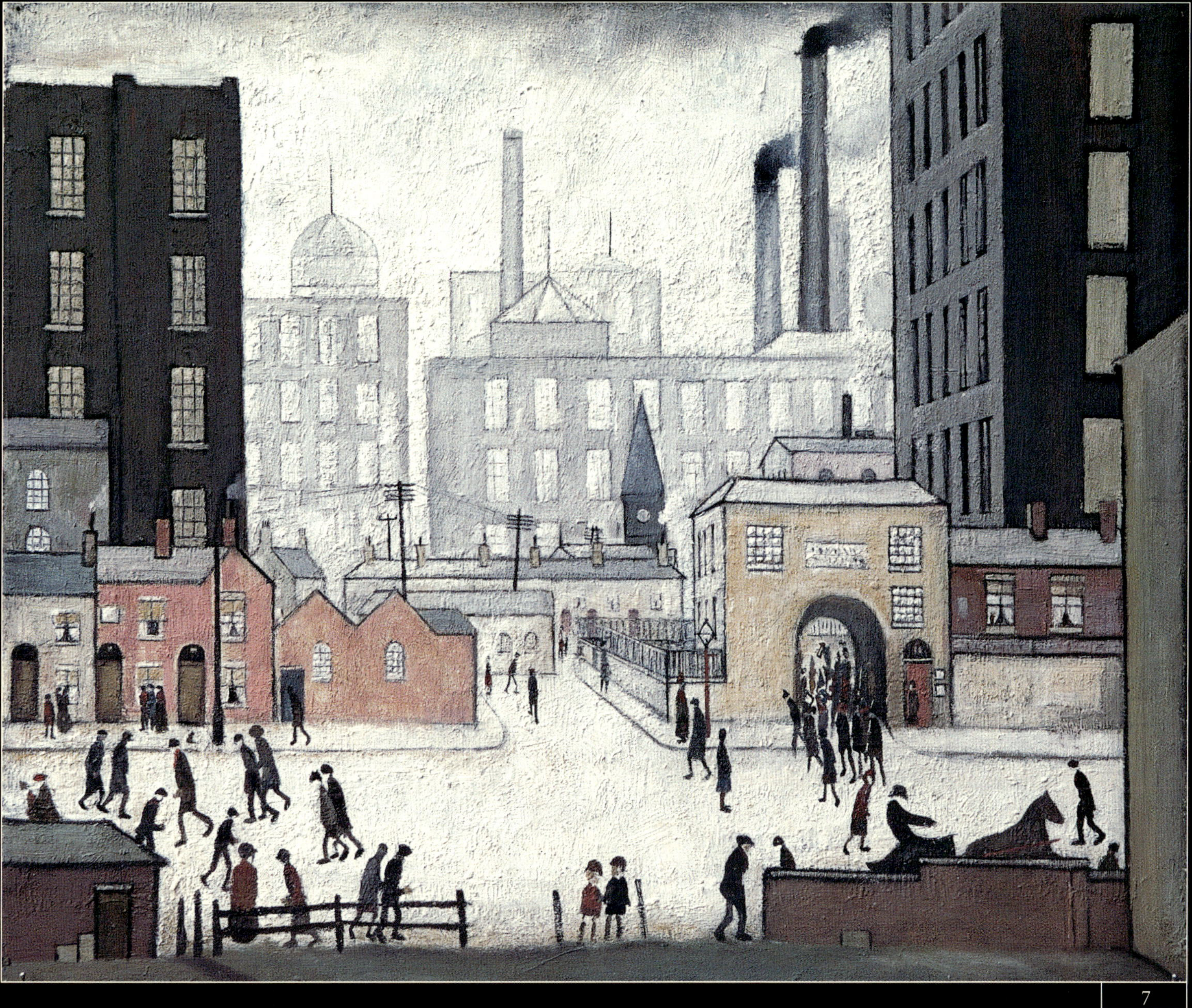

To paint figures dressed in garments of only one colour Lowry may have begun with a single curved stroke. But where a female figure wears a pullover and skirt he would paint the skirt first then, when this was dry, would partially scumble the pullover over the top. As the foreground filled up, to accurately locate other figures in the remaining available space, he may have begun with a cap or head, before adding the body, then the ochre legs, and finally two touches of black paint for the boots and a tiny smudge of pale pink ochre for the face. The tiniest touch of misplaced paint can alter the tilt of a cap - thereby changing a figure's entire bearing or the direction in which he or she looks.

He would continue to add small strokes of colour as the painting progressed, sometimes using a pointed sable brush for the legs.

In parts of the sky Lowry applied the paint with the flat blade of a palette knife, drawing it back from the surface to produce a stippled effect.

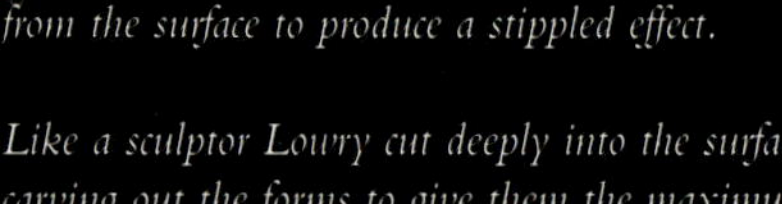

Like a sculptor Lowry cut deeply into the surface carving out the forms to give them the maximum degree of uncompromising actuality.

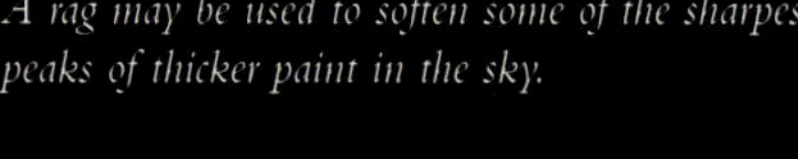

A rag may be used to soften some of the sharpest peaks of thicker paint in the sky.

As it neared completion Lowry probably felt that his picture looked too "fresh". To achieve quickly the "aged" look he preferred, he used his fingers to apply thin scumbles of paint, depositing the tiniest flecks of scarcely perceptible colour on the ridges of the heavily textured brushstrokes beneath. Tiny specks of black paint resemble particles of black soot floating in the smoke filled air and a thin rime of yellow ochre lies over the chalky pale green foreground.

The completed reconstruction. As Lowry's painting is more than seventy years old and covered in a thin layer of surface dirt, the reconstruction has a

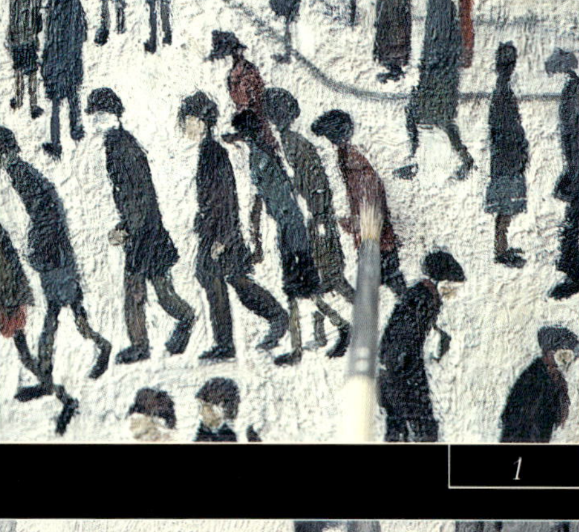

1

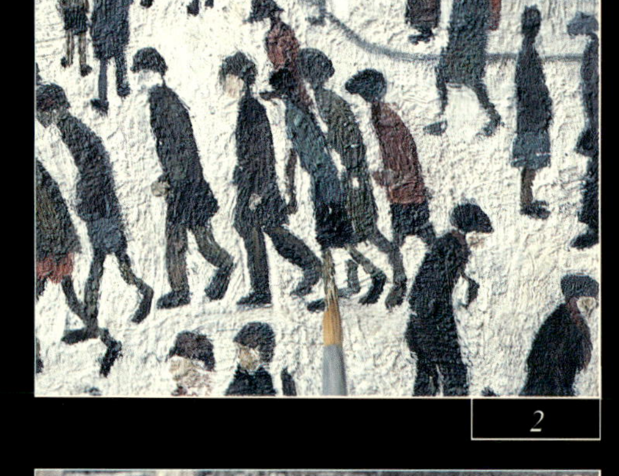

2

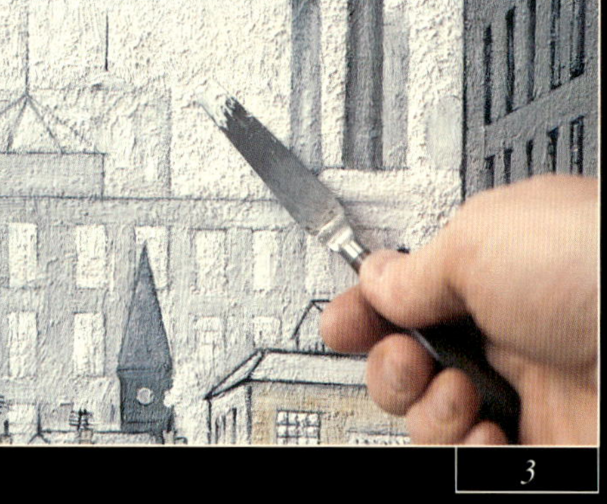

3

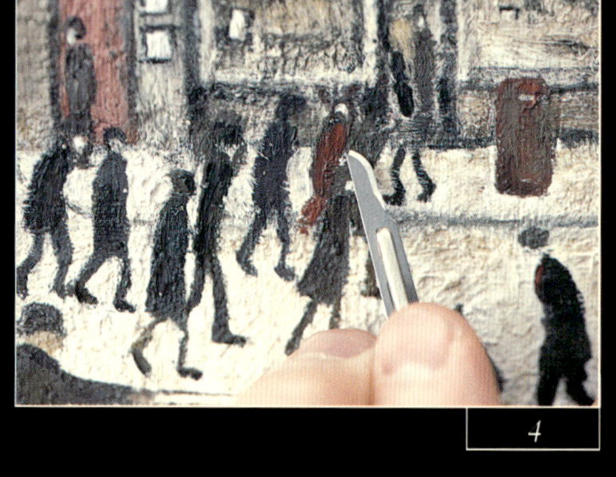

4

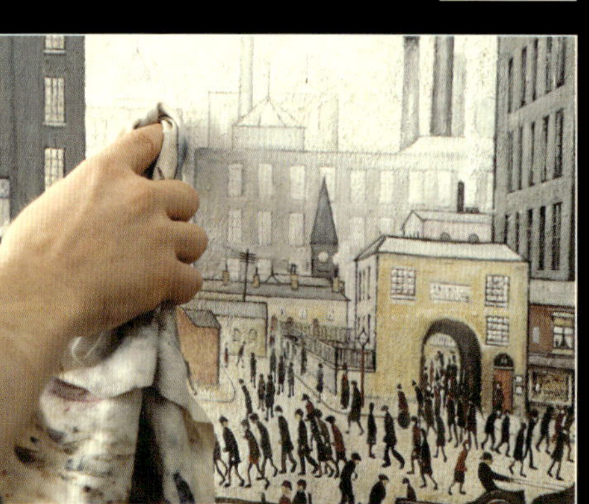

5

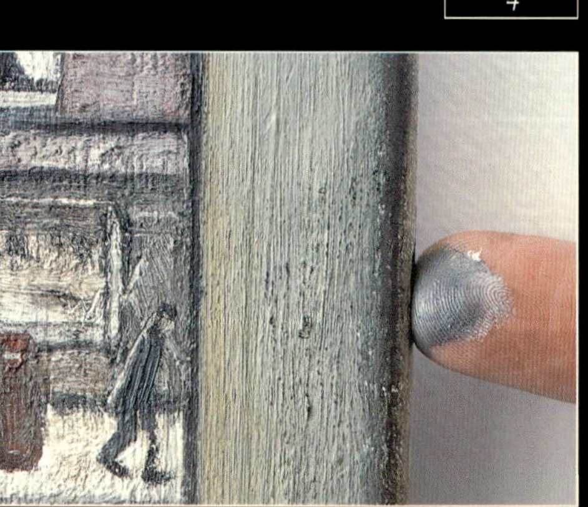

6

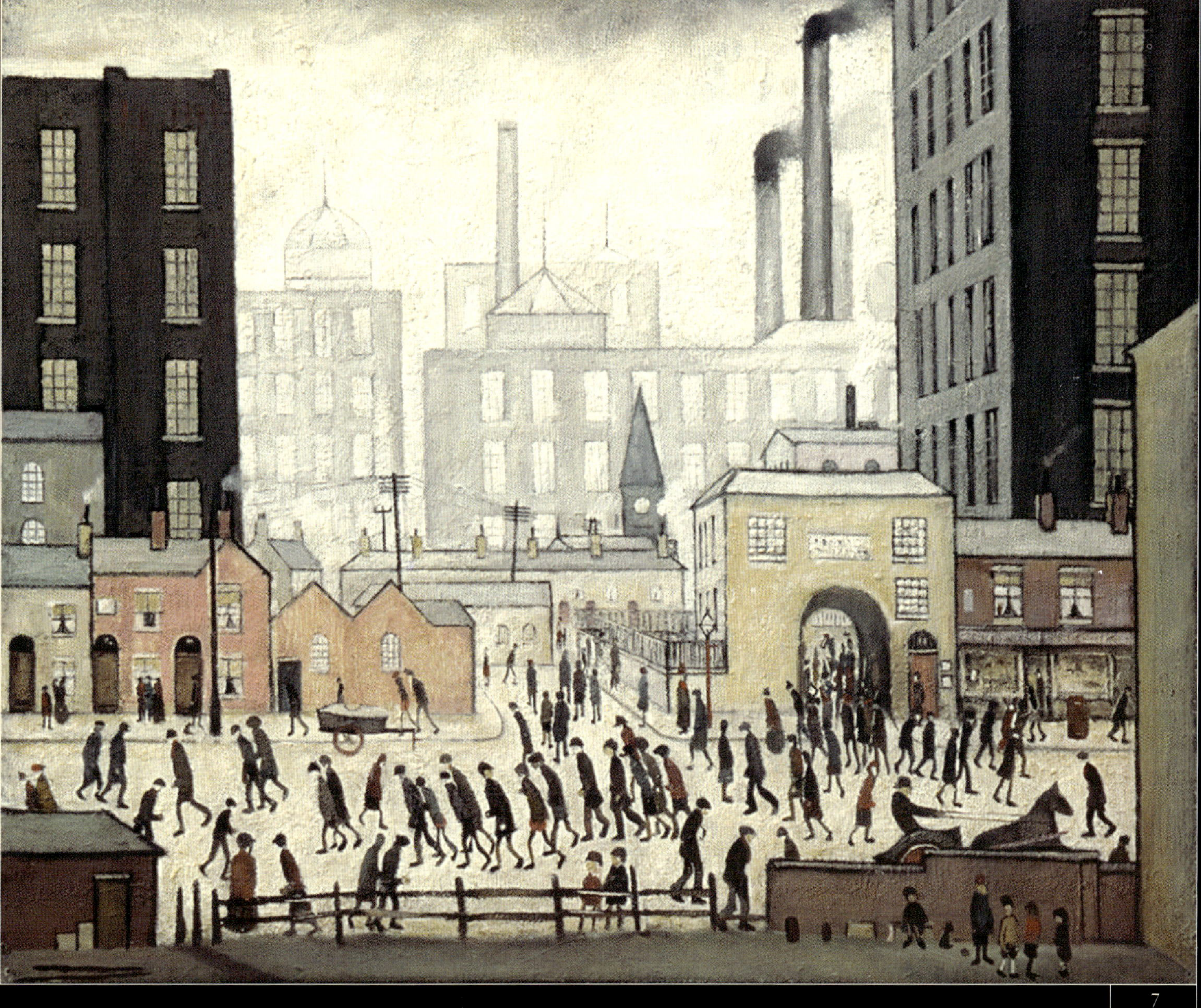

NOTES

1 L. S. Lowry to photographer Sefton Samuels, on tape, 1970.
When Sefton Samuels quizzed him: "I think somebody once said you take a great deal of trouble finding out the chemical composition of paints?" Lowry replied: "Never."
2 Allen Andrews, *The Life of L. S. Lowry,* 1977, p 19.
3 L. S. Lowry to Professor Hugh B Maitland, on tape, 1970.
4 Maitland tapes.
5 Andrews, p 53. Andrews suggests that it could have been *A Manufacturing Town,* 1922, but Lowry told his friend Professor Hugh Maitland that he showed Taylor "two pictures of dark figures on an absolutely white ground" (Maitland tapes).
6 Considering its quality, it is surprising that it was omitted from Lowry's first one-man show in London at the Reid and Lefevre Gallery in 1939.
7 Andrews, p 46.
8 Letter of 19 October 1956, quoted by M. Leber and J. Sandling in *L. S. Lowry,* 1987, p 109.
9 L. S. Lowry to Gerald B. Cotton, Chief Librarian of Swinton and Pendlebury and later Salford, and Frank Mullineux, Keeper of Monks Hall Museum, Eccles, on tape (undated).
10 Samuels tapes.
11 "Artists' Prepared Canvases from Winsor and Newton 1928–1951" by R. D. Harley in *Studies in Conservation, Vol 32, No 2,* May 1987, p 78.
12 Mullineux tapes.
13 See Julian Spalding, Lowry, 1979, p 10. Spalding was the first to note this phenomenon.
14 Mervyn Levy, *The Paintings of L. S. Lowry (Oils and Watercolours),* 1975, p 11. Lowry reiterated the point when discussing his painting in Birmingham Museum and Art Gallery entitled *An Industrial Town* which "... was painted on canvas... over a background of flake white dry, and my colours are and always have been flake white, ivory black, scarlet vermilion, Prussian blue and yellow ochre. Winsor and Newton's Artists' Colours and I have never used any medium at all ever..." (*Studies in Conservation, Vol 21,* No 1, February 1976, p 28).
15 Maitland tapes: "It was Fitz who caused Lowry to use a simple palette of primary colours. He had an array of colours which Fitz told him he did not need and advised him to discard." Another 20th-century artist who used three colours plus black and white is Piet Mondrian. Sir Joshua Reynolds similarly restricted his palette in the 18th century.
16 In conversation with Frank Mullineux and Gerald Cotton, Lowry described Titanium as "dangerous", adding that "It flakes; it cracks." As ever, he tried to throw questioners off the scent, for this is more likely to be the case with zinc white.
17 R. J. Gettens and G. L. Stout, *Painting Materials: A Short Encyclopaedia,* 1942, reprinted 1966, p 175.
18 *A Few Notes on the Composition and Permanence of Artists' Colours,* published by Winsor and Newton, Harrow, 1941, p 8. Zinc white became available as an artist's colour in the mid-19th century. It is a fairly opaque, non-toxic, cool white pigment (zinc white paste is used as an ointment). When dry the paint film tends to be brittle and prone to cracking. It does not dry as rapidly as white lead and its hiding power is lower than white lead or titanium white. To overcome these disadvantages it is sometimes mixed with white lead. Lowry never mentioned using zinc white but he may have used it when he was unable to obtain white lead.
19 In 1926, A. P. Laurie, Professor of Chemistry to the Royal Academy, published his book entitled *The Painter's Methods and Materials.* On pages 136 to 139 he describes a number of experiments he carried out into the yellowing of flake white and zinc white when mixed with a number of different oils and other mediums. He found that moisture as well as darkness hastens the rate of yellowing. It is not known whether Lowry owned or knew of this book.
20 Gettens and Stout, p 150.
21 Winsor and Newton, Harrow, 1941, p 8.

L. S. Lowry's *Coming from the Mill* is in the Lowry Collection housed at The Lowry, Pier 8, Salford Quays M50 3AZ www.thelowry.com

Edwin Bowes' reconstruction of the painting was initiated by The Lowry.

Photographic Acknowledgements
All process photographs are © Ben Blackall, whose assistance with the project is gratefully acknowledged.

© Salford University: p 2
© Private collection: p 4
© The Lowry Collection, City of Salford: p 6, 7, 9, 13, 18
© The Lowry Estate: p 8, 10

Publishing and editorial direction by Roger Sears
Edited by Michael Leitch
Designed by Martin Tilley at Pocknell Studio

Published by the Lowry Press

The Lowry, Pier 8, Salford Quays, M50 3AZ

First published 2002

© The Lowry Centre Limited

A CIP catalogue record for this book is available from The British Library

ISBN 1-902970-26-8

Originated in Hong Kong and printed and bound in Spain by Imago